NILES - TEMPLESMITH - MENTON3

LUST

M3

STEVE NILES - writer

Steve Niles is a writer. He writes comics, novels and films. Best known for works such as *30 Days of Night, Criminal Macabre, Simon Dark, Mystery Society* and *Batman: Gotham County Line*, he is credited among other contemporary writers as bringing horror comics back to prominence.

Niles is currently working for four of the top American comic publishers - IDW, DC, Image and Dark Horse. Everyone's favorite monster hunter Cal McDonald continues in the *Criminal Macabre* series from Dark Horse, as well as in stories currently being published by Steve's own Bloody Pulp Books.

The success of *30 Days of Night* sparked renewed interest in the horror genre; Steve's comic was released as a major motion picture in 2007 with Spider Man's Sam Raimi producing, David Slade directing, and Niles co-writing the screenplay. Other comics he has written that have been optioned for film include *Criminal Macabre* and *Aleister Arcane*, as well as *Wake the Dead*, with Jay Russell in the director's chair.

Currently, Steve is writing *Chin Music* for Image Comics. Niles is also working on *Frankenstein 2 Alive! Alive!* with the legendary Bernie Wrightson. Wrightson has also illustrated Niles' *Doc Macabre, The Ghoul*, and *Dead She Said* series, all published by IDW. Just released, *A Glimpse of Crime and Terror* with Scott Morse, as well as *Edge of Doom*, with Kelley Jones. Steve also released a free digital prequel to *The Thing* through Dark Horse Comics. Niles' zombie comic, *Remains*, was released as part of Chiller Network's "Chiller Presents" series in December 2011 and is available on DVD and BluRay.

Steve was raised in the Washington, D.C. suburbs, developing his interests in music, writing, and making amateur films. He worked in several comic book stores and played in the bands Gray Matter and Three during the heyday of the Washington harDCore punk scene. Both bands released records on the Dischord Records label.

Niles got his start in the comic industry when he formed his own publishing company called Arcane Comix, where he published, edited, and adapted several comics and anthologies for Eclipse Comics. His adaptations include works by Clive Barker, Richard Matheson, and Harlan Ellison. IDW released a hardcover and softcover collection of Niles' adaptation of Richard Matheson's *I Am Legend*.

Steve resides in Austin, Texas with his fiancé Monica, two dogs, four cats, and Gill the tortoise. While there's no crawlspace, there is a questionable closet in one corner and no one is quite sure what is hidden in there... but we have an idea.

BEN TEMPLESMITH – artist

Ben Templesmith is a *New York Times* best selling artist and writer most widely known for his work in the comic book industry where he has received multiple nominations for the International Horror Guild Awards as well as the industry's top prize, the Eisner Award. He also won a Spike TV Scream Award.

He was born March 7, 1984 in Perth, Australia, was raised as an orphan by monks, and studied marine biology and design at UWA.

As a creator, his most notable works have been *30 Days of Night* (which spawned a major motion picture) and *Fell*. His other projects include the critically acclaimed serial *Wormwood: Gentleman Corpse*, as well as *Welcome to Hoxford* and *Singularity 7*, all of which he also wrote.

He's also worked on *Star Wars, Doctor Who, GI Joe, Army of Darkness, Silent Hill*, and, among others.

He does art for money in a strange thing some would call a "career" and follows the Giant Space Squid. He spends his time in both Chicago and New York City. Ben is co-founder of 44FLOOD.

MENTON3 - artist

Menton J. Matthews III aka menton3 is a writer, fine artist, and illustrator. His techniques and subjects draw heavily from old masterworks, alchemical writings, symbology, and Jungian psychology. He is Co-Founder and Chief Creative Officer of 44FLOOD.

His comic book work includes being co-creator/artist of *Transfusion* at IDW and *The Nosferatu Wars* at Dark Horse, both with writer Steve Niles. He was also co-creator/writer and artist of *MONOCYTE*, series artist for *Silent Hill: Past Life*, interior artist for *Zombies vs. Robots: Aventure*, and cover/interior artist for *HP Lovecraft's The Dunwich Horror*, all at IDW. He is a sought-after cover artist, including covers for *The Thing, Proof, Teenage Mutant Ninja Turtles, The Classics Mutilated, 30 Days of Night*, and more. Illustration work has included art for *The Lovecraft Library: Out of Arkham* and *Mark Twain's Tales of Mystery*, both from IDW. He is Co-Creator/Designer, as well as a Featured Artist in *TOME 1 - Vampirism* and is Co-Creator/Editor/Designer, as well as Featured Artist in *EXPLICITUS EST LIBER 1*, both from 44FLOOD.

His creator-owned graphic novel series, *Ars Memoria*, is a story of how a man's quest to resolve the singular tragic event of his past ends up leading him face first with the darkest recesses of himself.

His fine art paintings have been shown in prominent galleries including La Luz de Jesus, Strychnin Gallery, and Last Rites. He has also enjoyed a career as a professional musician/recording engineer, founding the band Sunday Munich and creating the solo project Saltillo. His newest musical project is called Paintings for the Flood with Richard Walters.

WARREN ELLIS - Foreword

Warren Ellis is the award-winning writer of graphic novels like *Transmetropolitan, Fell, Ministry of Space*, and *Planetary*, and the author of the "underground classic" novel *Crooked Little Vein*.

The movie *RED* is based on his graphic novel of the same name. His *Gravel* books are in development for film at Legendary Pictures, with Tim Miller attached to direct, and his novel *Gun Machine* has been bought by Chernin Entertainment for television. The *Iron Man 3* feature film is based on his Marvel Comics graphic novel *Iron Man: Extremis*.

He's also written extensively for *VICE, WIRED UK*, and *Reuters* on technological and cultural matters, and is co-writing a video project called *Wastelanders* with Joss Whedon. Warren is currently working on another novel for Mulholland Books, and a non-fiction book about the future of the city for Farrar Giroux Strauss. A documentary about his work, *Captured Ghosts*, was released in 2012.

Recognitions include the NUIG Literary and Debating Society's President's Medal for service to freedom of speech, the EAGLE AWARDS Roll Of Honour for lifetime achievement in the field of comics and graphic novels, the Grand Prix de l'Imaginaire 2010, the Sidewise Award for Alternate History, and the International Horror Guild Award for illustrated narrative.

Warren lives outside London, on the southeast coast of England, in case he needs to make a quick getaway.

KASRA GHANBARI - VICE Series Editor

Kasra Ghanbari is a writer, painter, art agent, and entrepreneur. He is Co-Founder and CEO of 44FLOOD.

Kasra was Co-Creator/Writer of *MONOCYTE*, an occult action-adventure comic book series from IDW Publishing. He was Co-Editor/Compiler and Publisher of *Drawing the Line Again*, a comic book anthology for cancer charity that included Hayao Miyazaki, Moebius, Bill Sienkiewicz, Dave Sims, and Clive Barker with 100% of proceeds going to The Princess Margaret Foundation and SickKids Foundation. The project raised over $80,000 and was nominated for a Shuster Award.

Most recently, Kasra was Co-Creator/Designer and Curator/Editor of *TOME 1 - Vampirism*, as well as Co-Creator/Editor/Designer of *EXPLICITUS EST LIBER 1*, both from 44FLOOD.

For the last decade, Kasra has been artist agent to both up-and-coming and established artists in the fine art and comic book fields. Artists represented have included Clive Barker, Scott Radke, Ted McKeever, menton3, Guillermo Rigattieri, and Richard A. Kirk.

In 1999, Kasra founded Panacea Pharmaceuticals, Inc. in Rockville, Maryland serving as President, COO, and member of the Board of Directors. Panacea focuses on developing therapeutics/diagnostics for diseases with substantial unmet clinical need, specifically cancer, stroke, Alzheimer's disease, and Parkinson's disease. Prior to Panacea, Kasra helped start Nymox Pharmaceutical Corporation (NASDAQ: NYMX) in Montreal, Quebec. He served as Project Leader for Alzheimer's Diagnostic Development, responsible for developing the AD7C test, an Alzheimer's Disease diagnostic test that remains marketed throughout the world. Kasra has published nearly 40 scientific publications and abstracts in peer-reviewed journals.

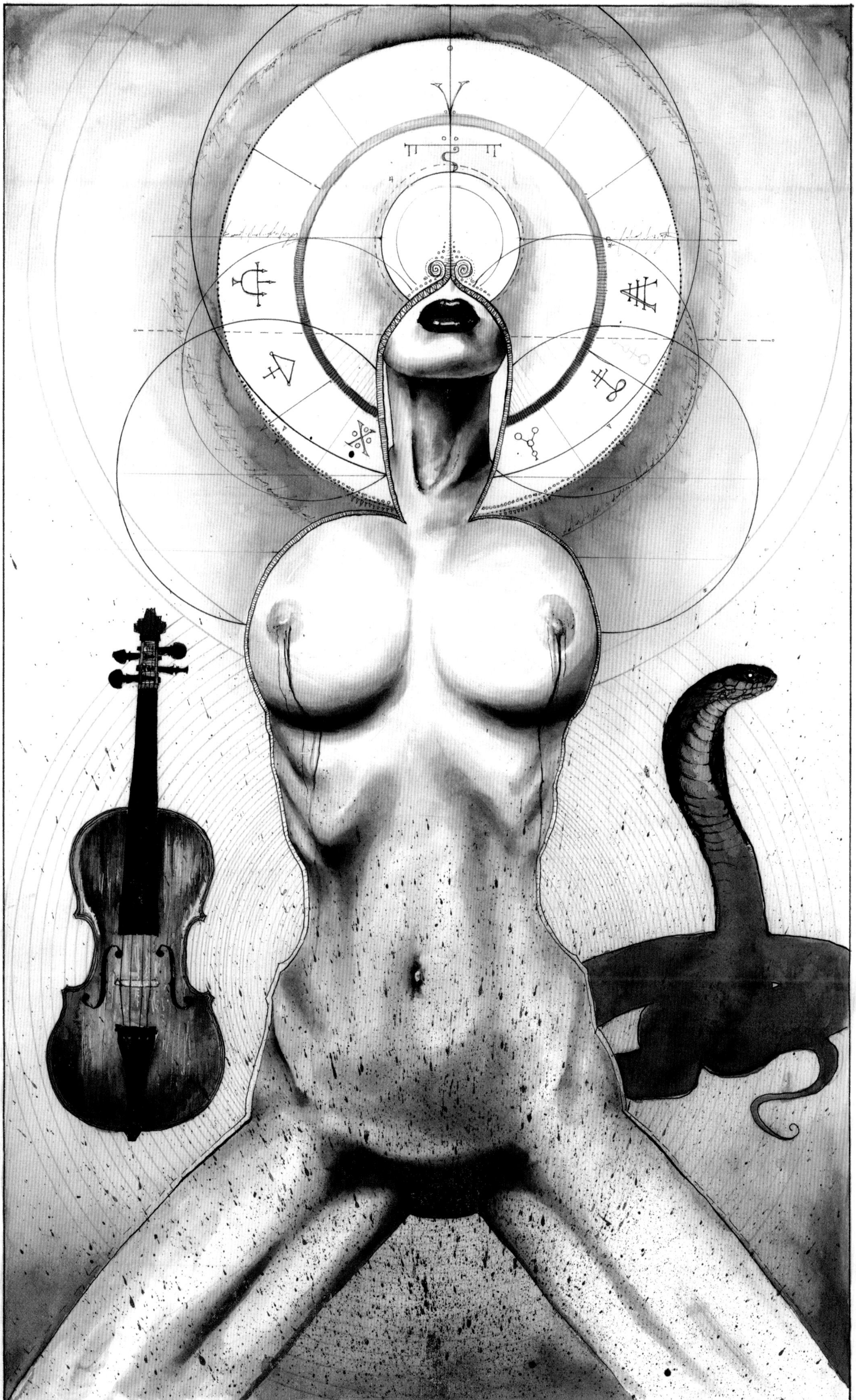

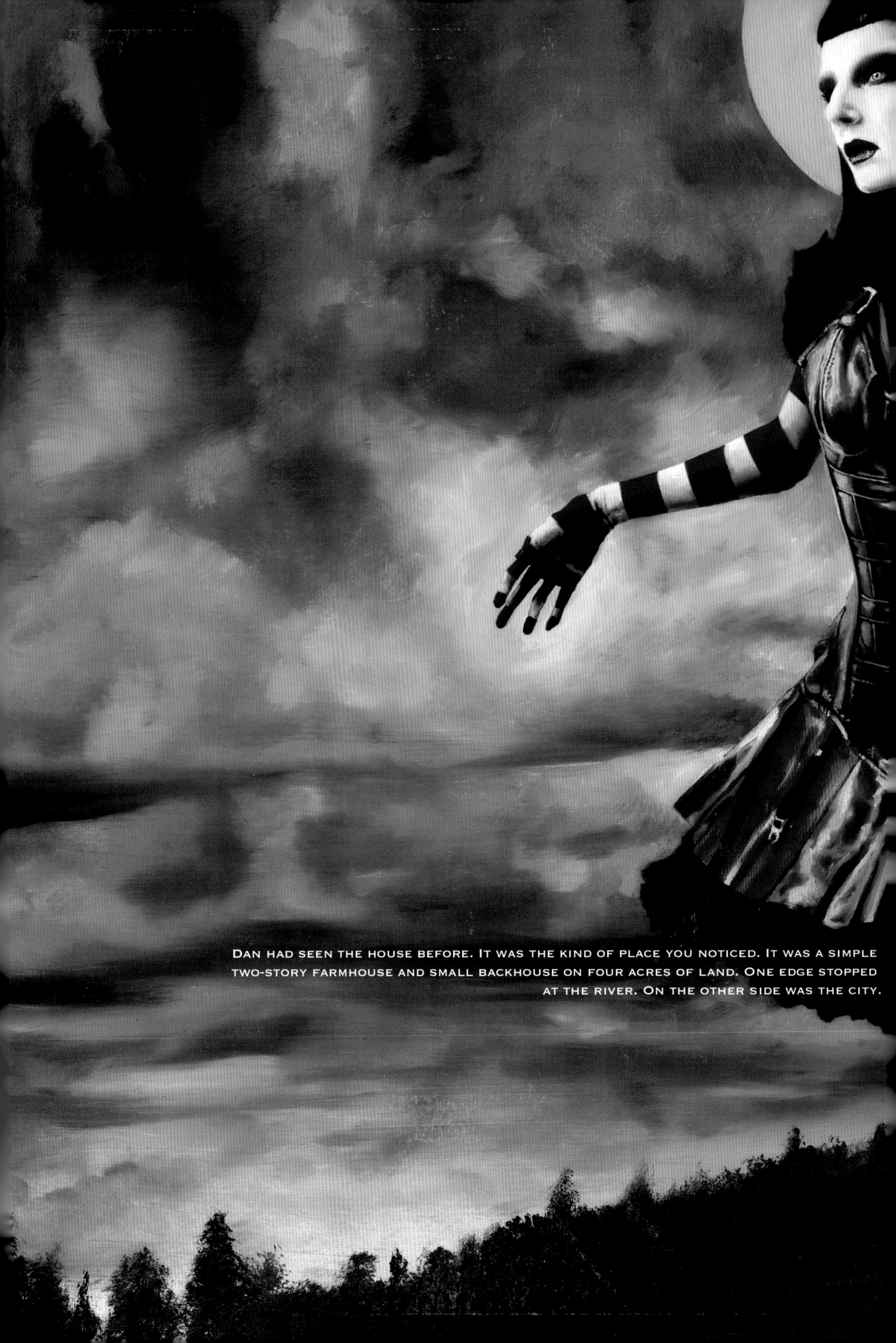

Dan had seen the house before. It was the kind of place you noticed. It was a simple two-story farmhouse and small backhouse on four acres of land. One edge stopped at the river. On the other side was the city.

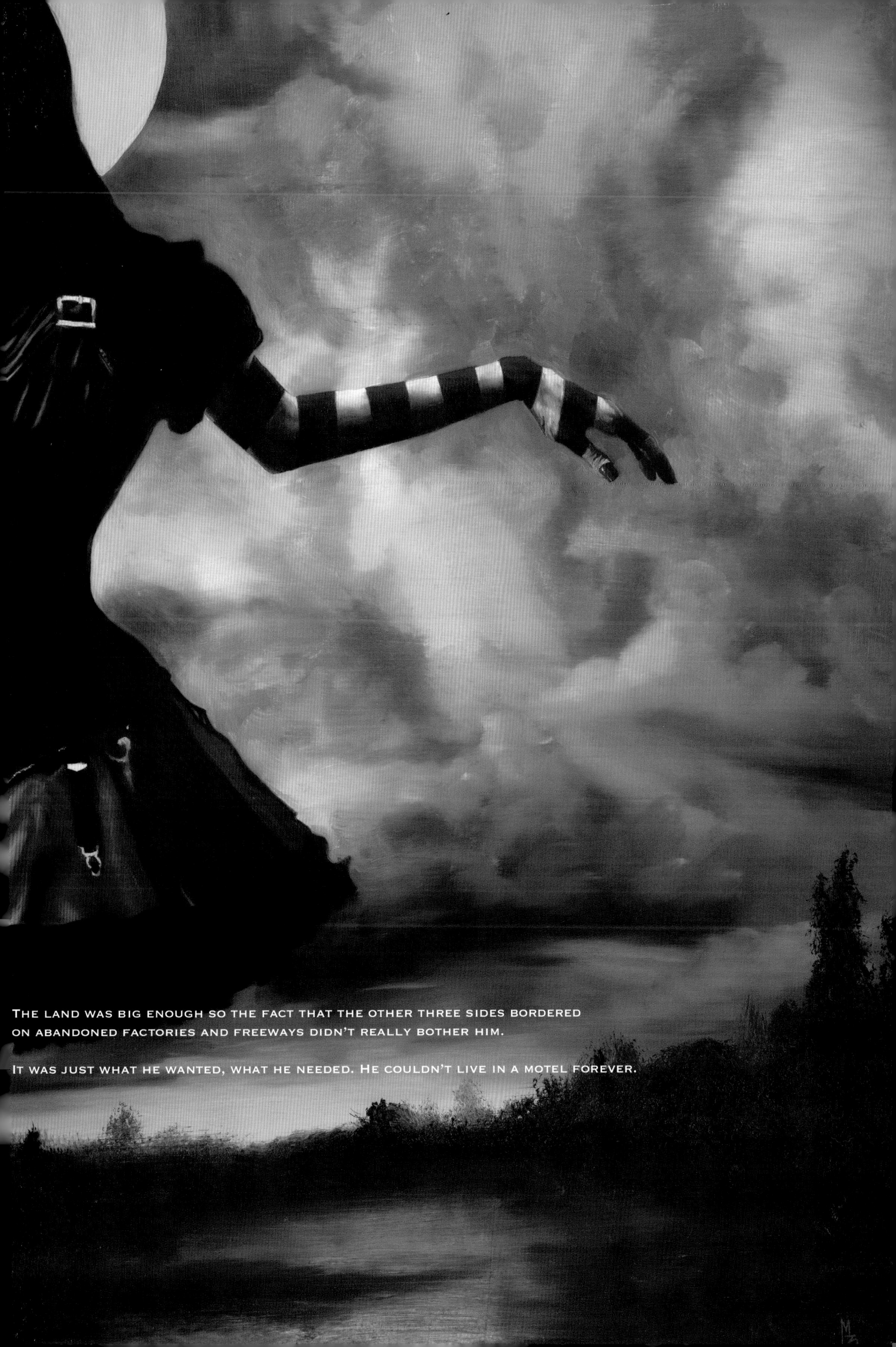

The land was big enough so the fact that the other three sides bordered on abandoned factories and freeways didn't really bother him.

It was just what he wanted, what he needed. He couldn't live in a motel forever.

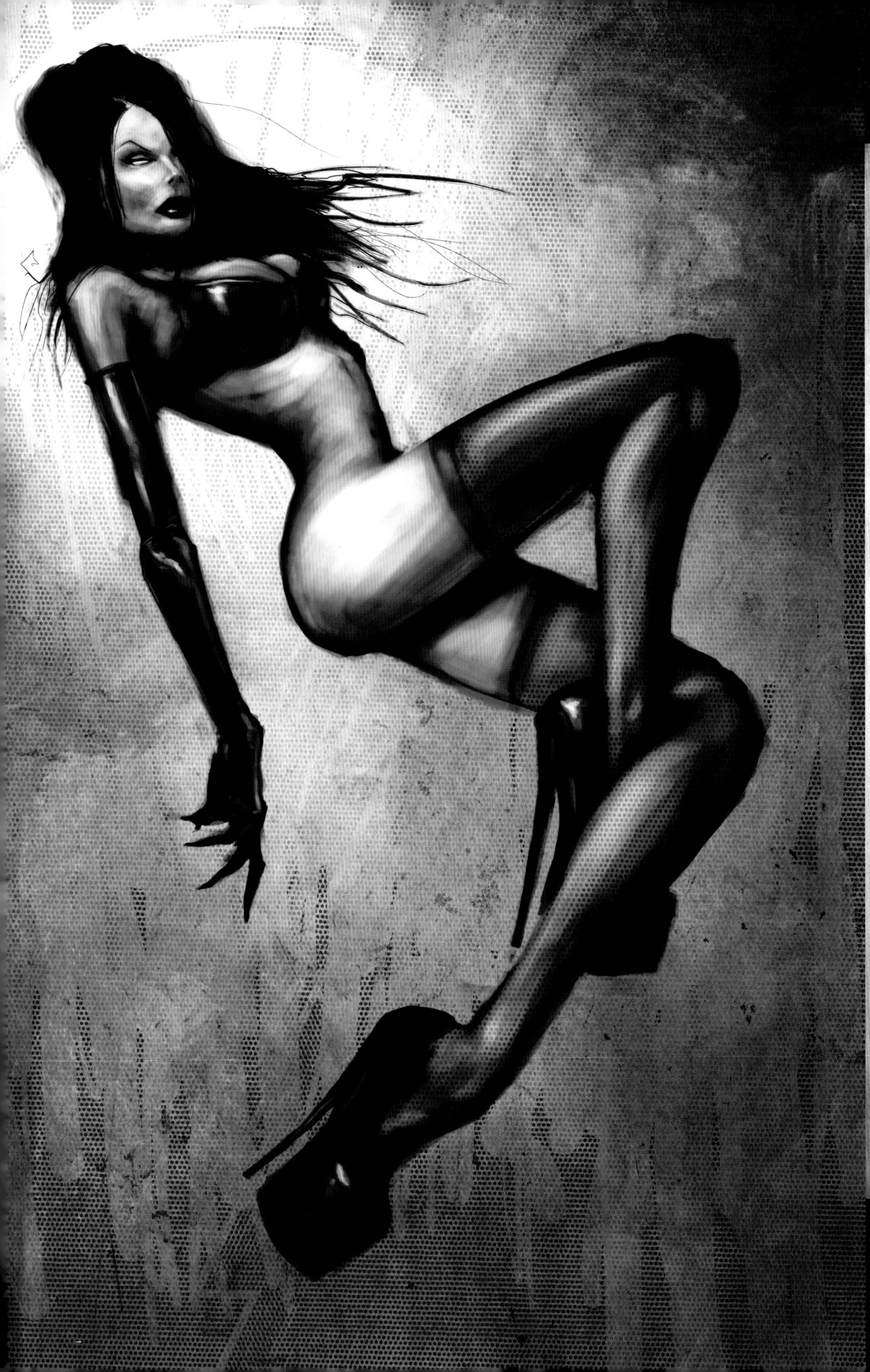

SHE GOT THE KIDS. NO MATTER HOW MANY TIMES HE TRIED TO MAKE SENSE OF IT,
DAN STILL COULDN'T BELIEVE THEY LET HER TAKE THEM AWAY FROM HIM.

HE CAUGHT HER FUCKING HER PARTNER. SHE'D COME HOME BRUISED AND BLOODY, STINKING OF HIM.

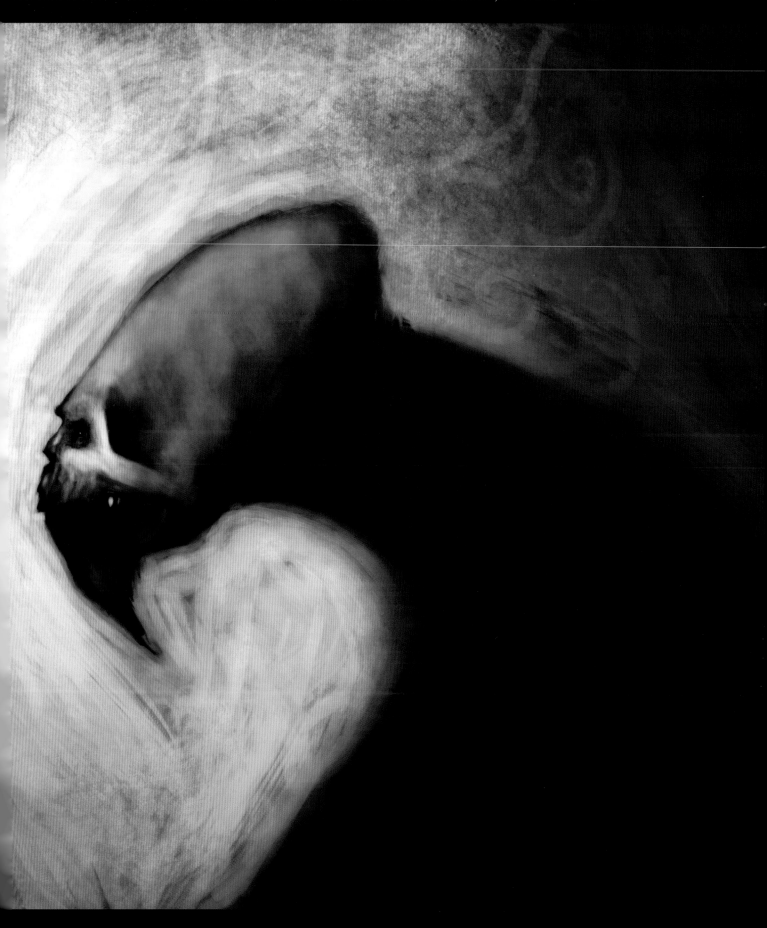

AND HE'S THE ONE WHO LOST CUSTODY. LOST EVERYTHING. EVERYTHING HE OWNED
WAS IN THE CAR PARKED IN FRONT OF THE HOUSE. HE STOOD IN THE YARD, DOWN
THE LONG DIRT ROAD, UNCEREMONIOUSLY REMOVING THE "SOLD" SIGN.

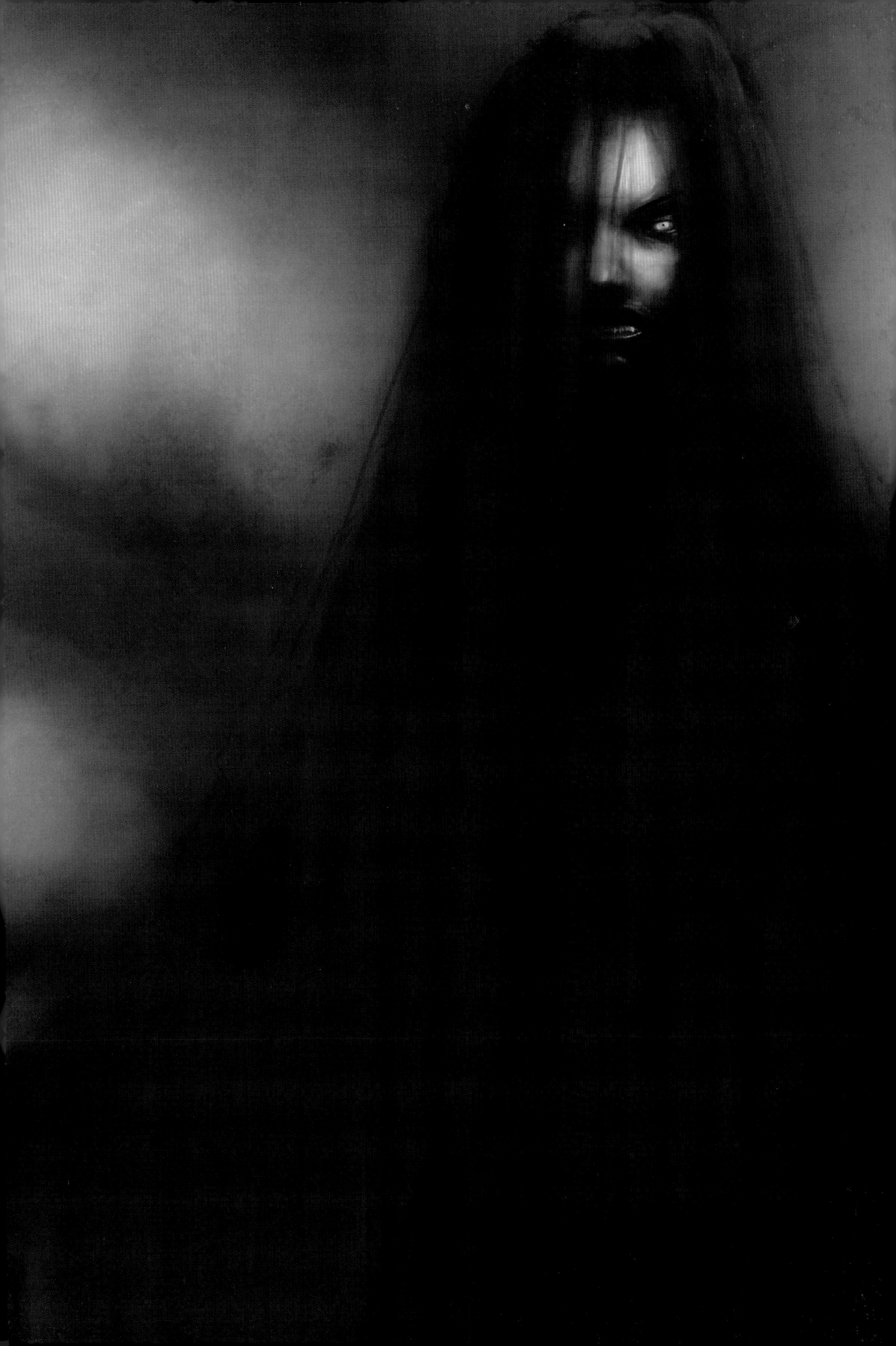

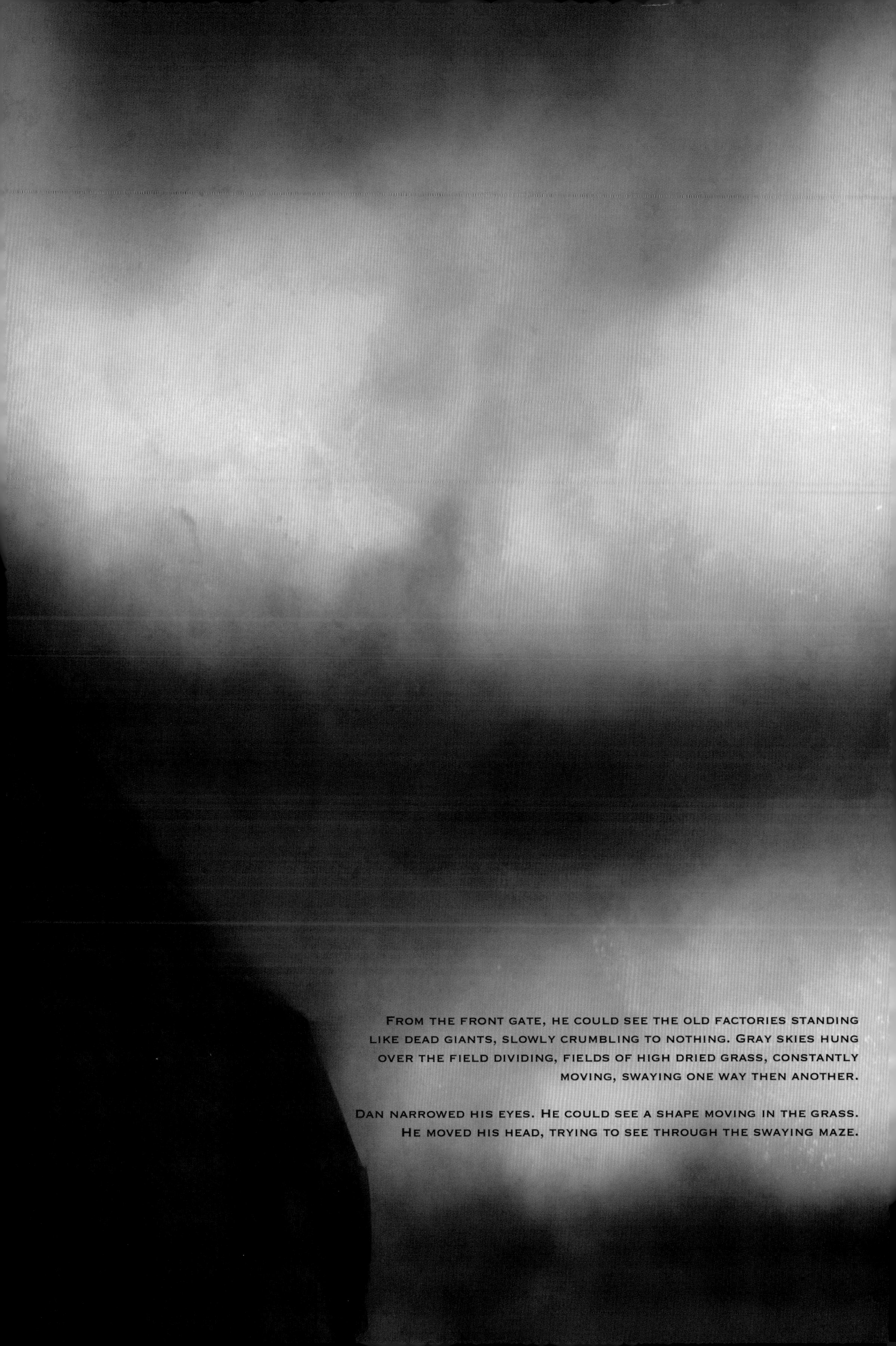

From the front gate, he could see the old factories standing like dead giants, slowly crumbling to nothing. Gray skies hung over the field dividing, fields of high dried grass, constantly moving, swaying one way then another.

Dan narrowed his eyes. He could see a shape moving in the grass. He moved his head, trying to see through the swaying maze.

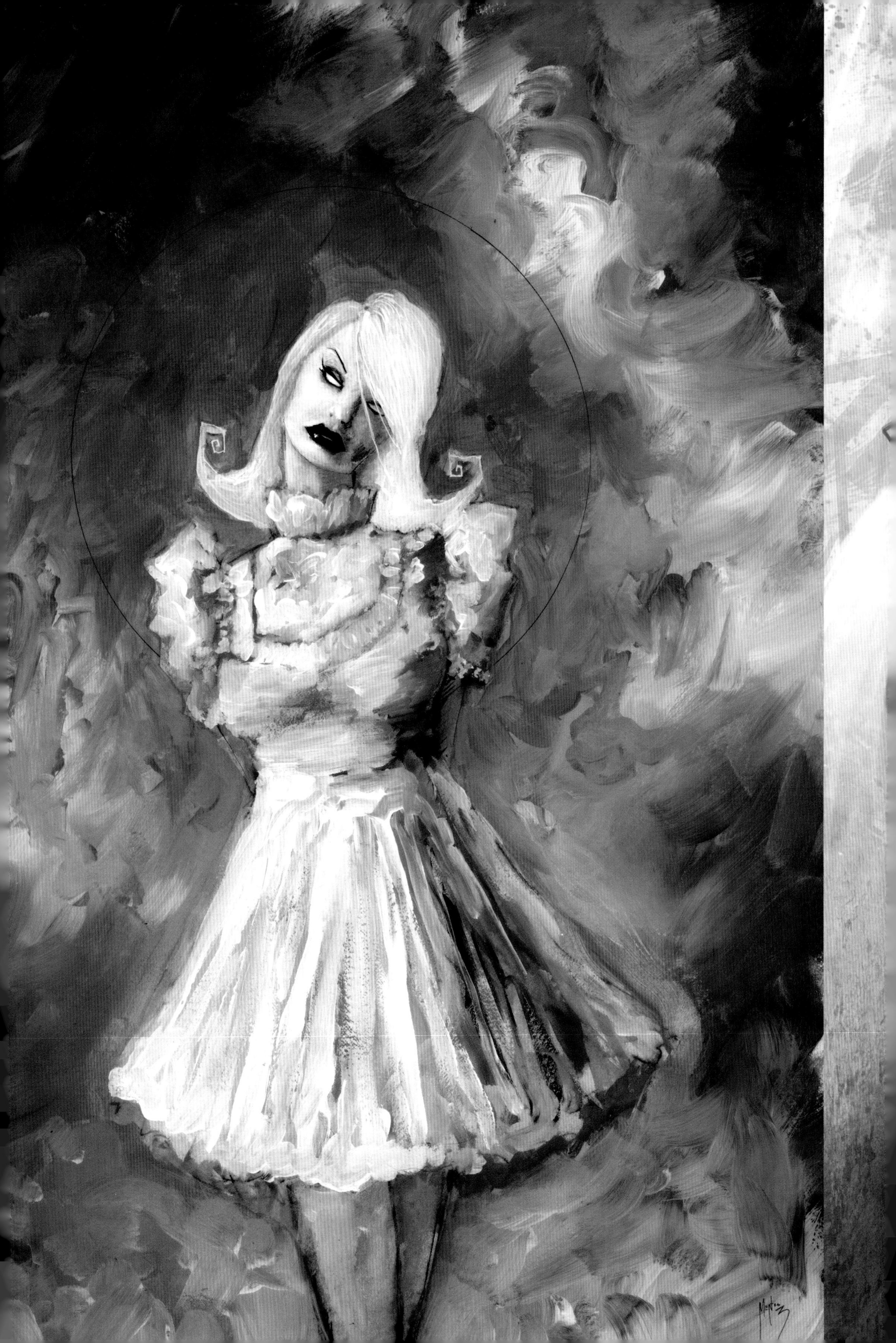

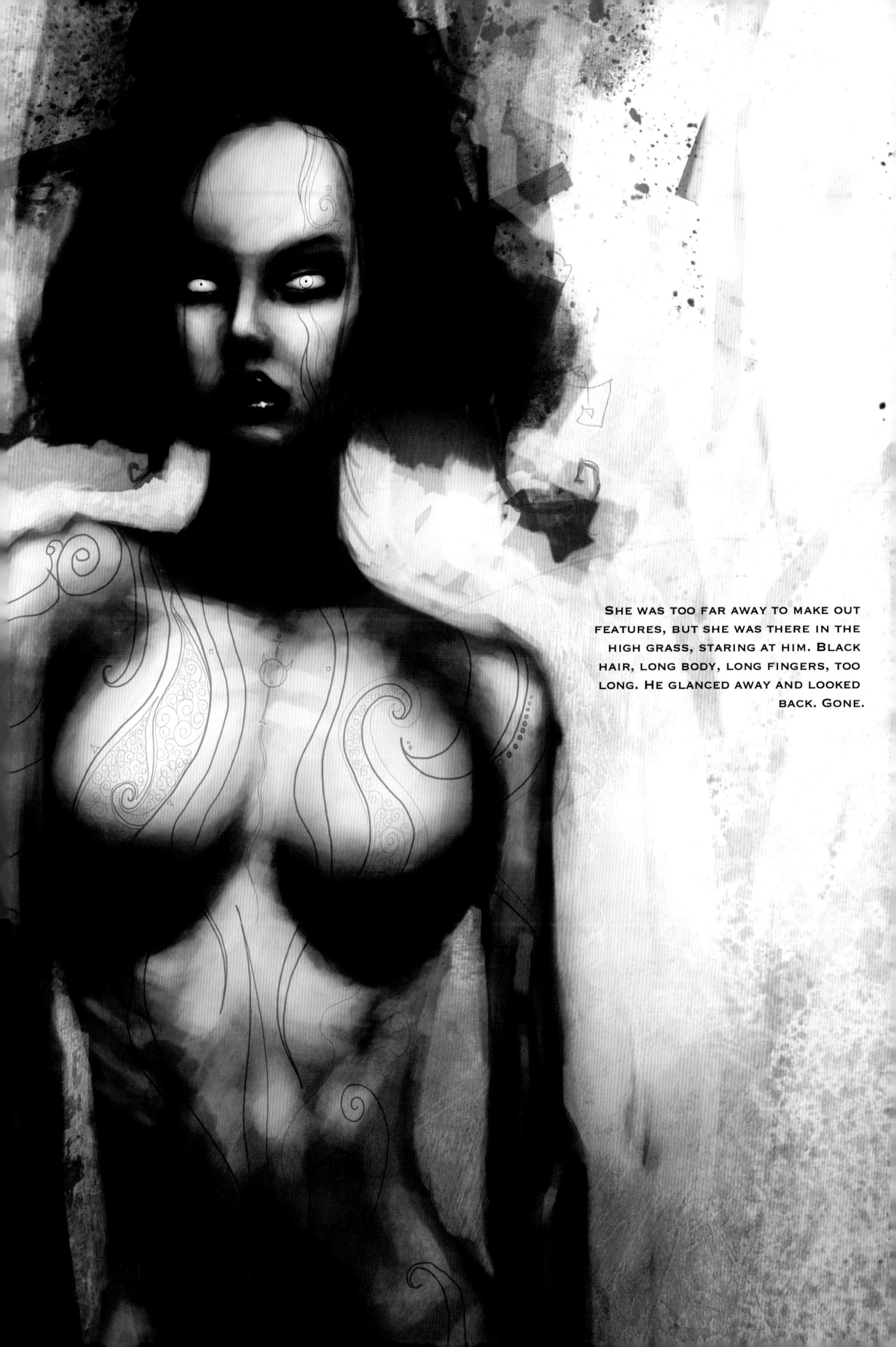

SHE WAS TOO FAR AWAY TO MAKE OUT FEATURES, BUT SHE WAS THERE IN THE HIGH GRASS, STARING AT HIM. BLACK HAIR, LONG BODY, LONG FINGERS, TOO LONG. HE GLANCED AWAY AND LOOKED BACK. GONE.

He carried the sign back to the house and leaned it against the car park wall. He grabbed the last of his belongings from the car, including his grandfather's easel. He paused at the front door, looking around at the expanse of gloomy nothing, then went inside.

Inside the house, he placed down the armful he carried and paused in front of an old mirror with coat hooks left behind by the former owners. He looked at his face a long time.

"You look like a fucking 'Dan.' Dan the dud. Dan the doormat."

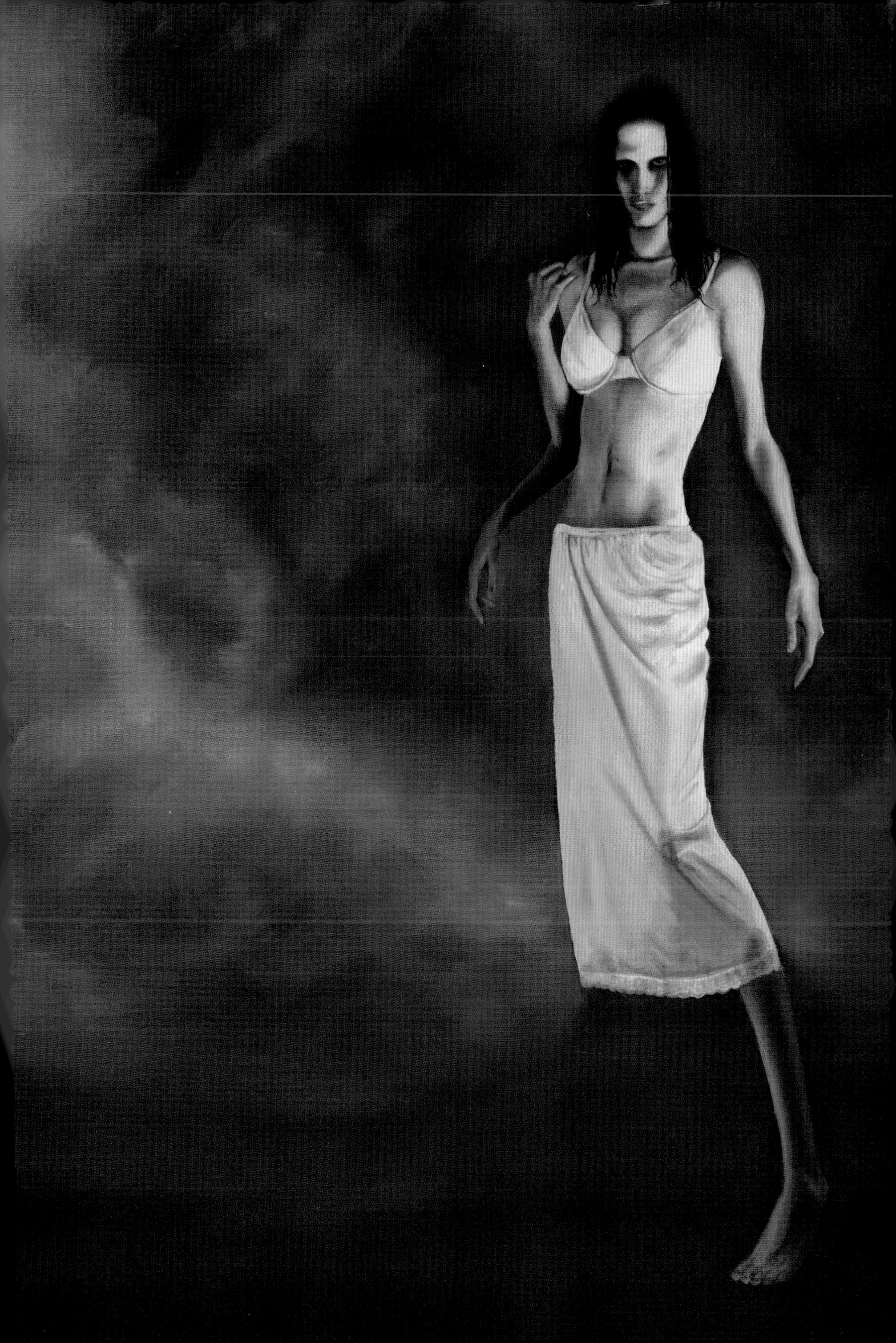

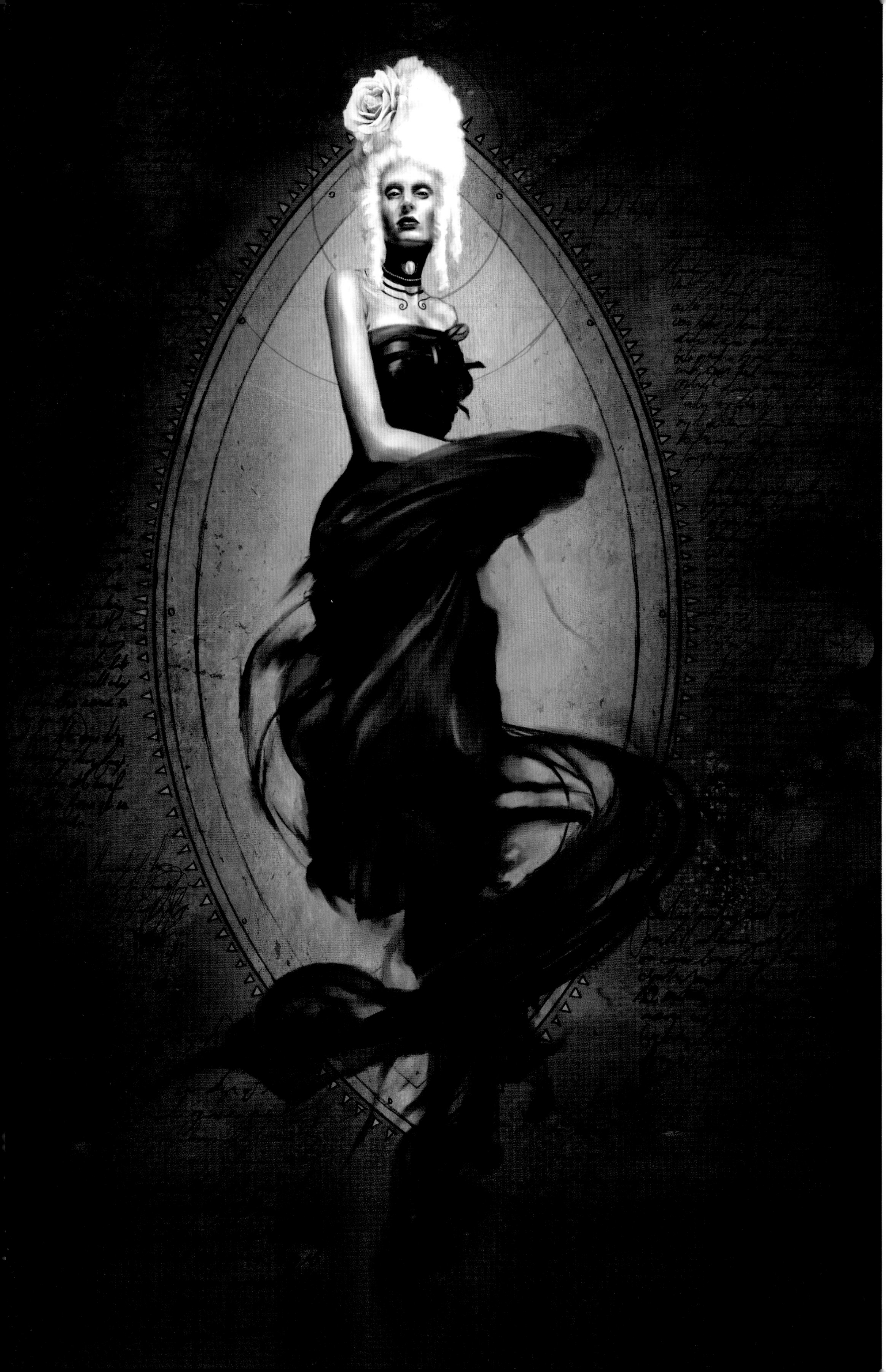

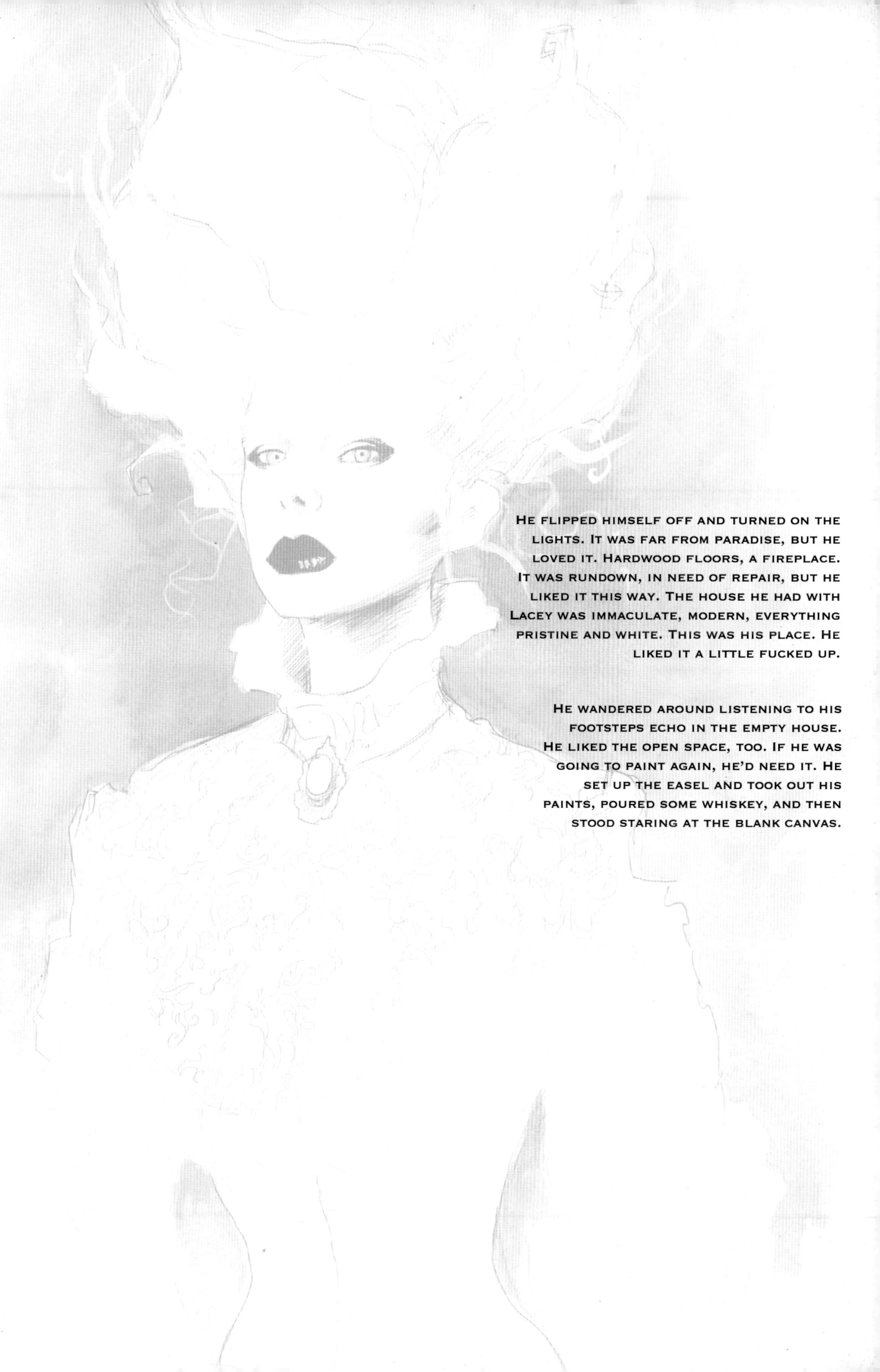

He flipped himself off and turned on the lights. It was far from paradise, but he loved it. Hardwood floors, a fireplace. It was rundown, in need of repair, but he liked it this way. The house he had with Lacey was immaculate, modern, everything pristine and white. This was his place. He liked it a little fucked up.

He wandered around listening to his footsteps echo in the empty house. He liked the open space, too. If he was going to paint again, he'd need it. He set up the easel and took out his paints, poured some whiskey, and then stood staring at the blank canvas.

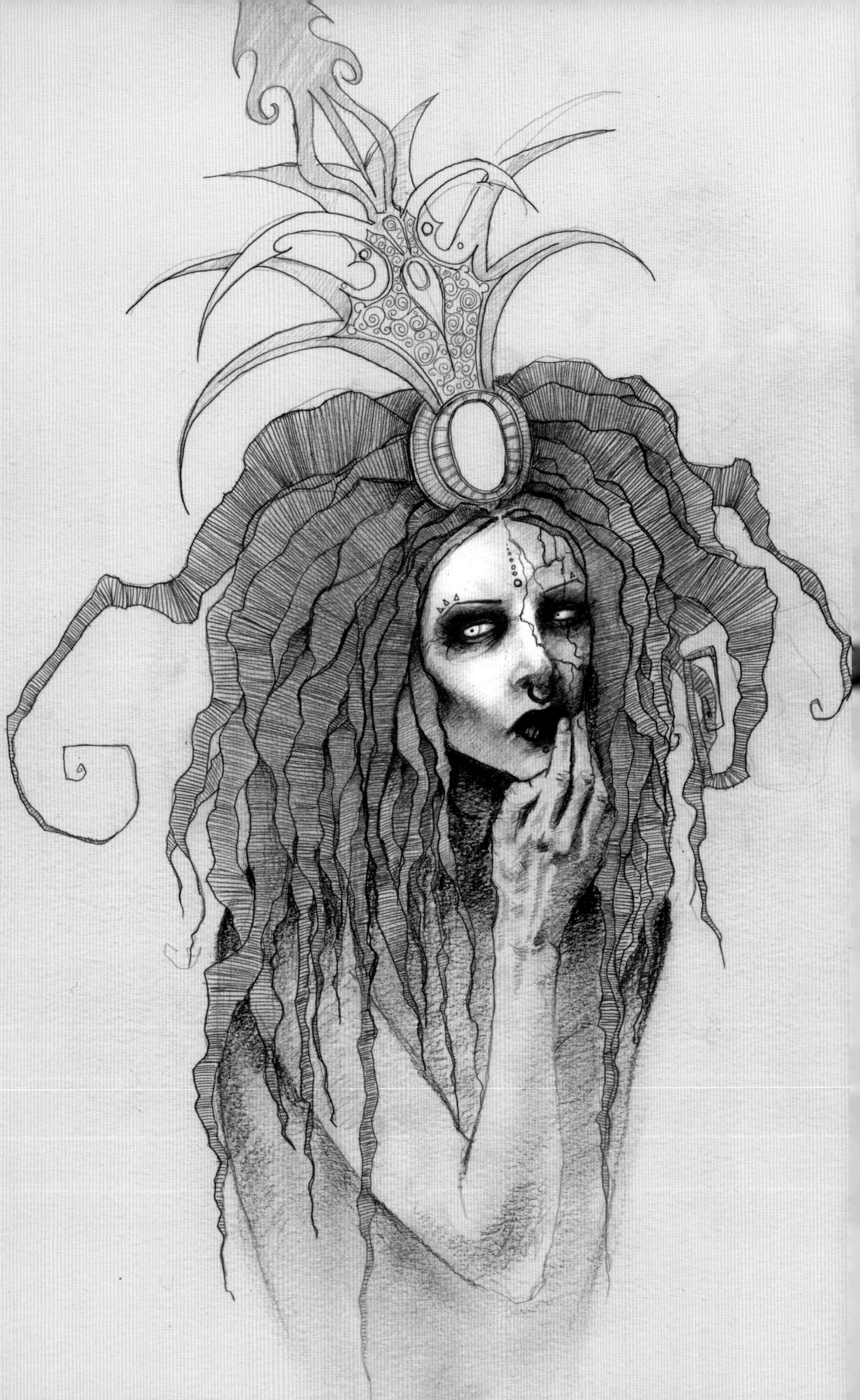

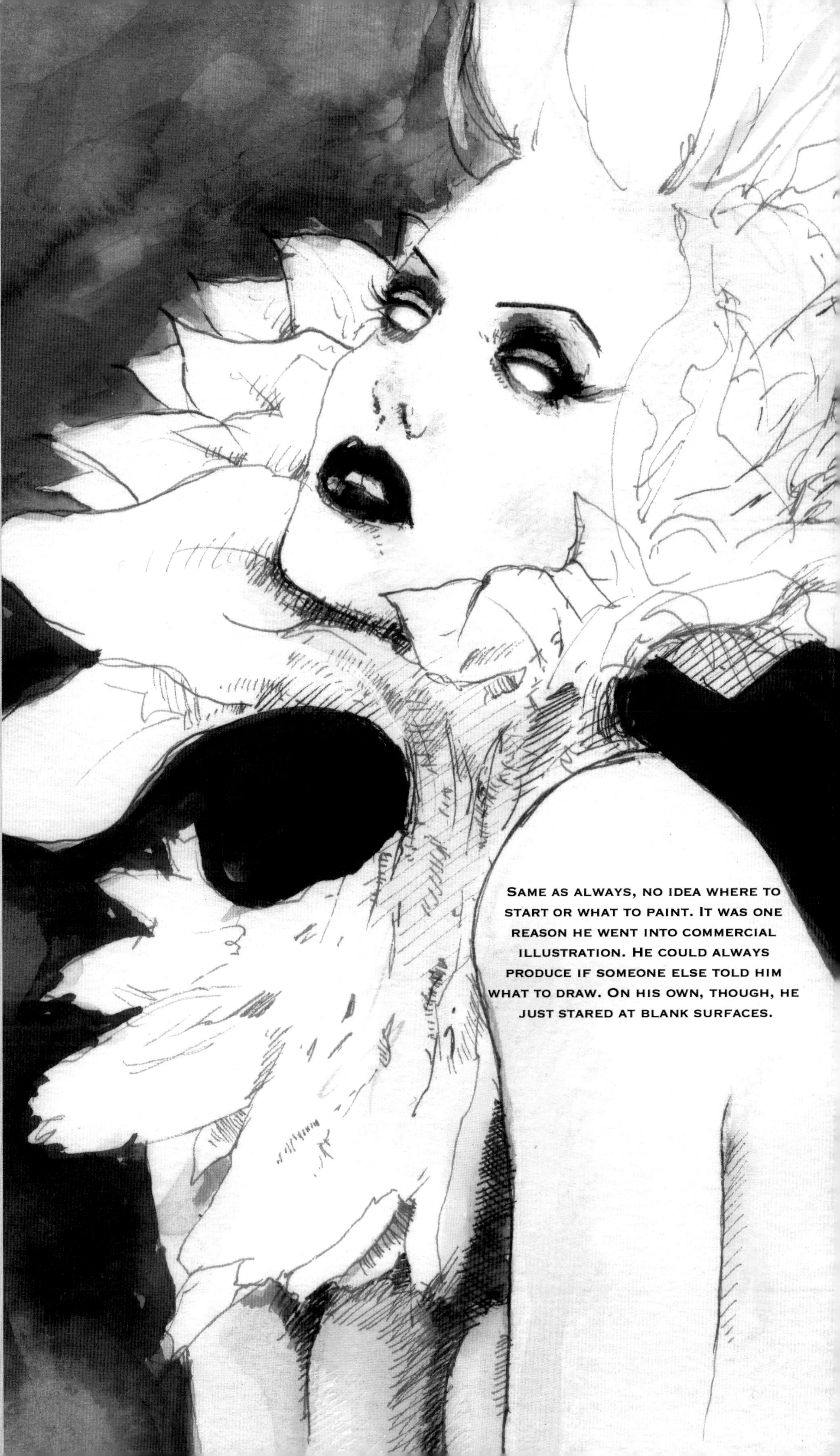
Same as always, no idea where to start or what to paint. It was one reason he went into commercial illustration. He could always produce if someone else told him what to draw. On his own, though, he just stared at blank surfaces.

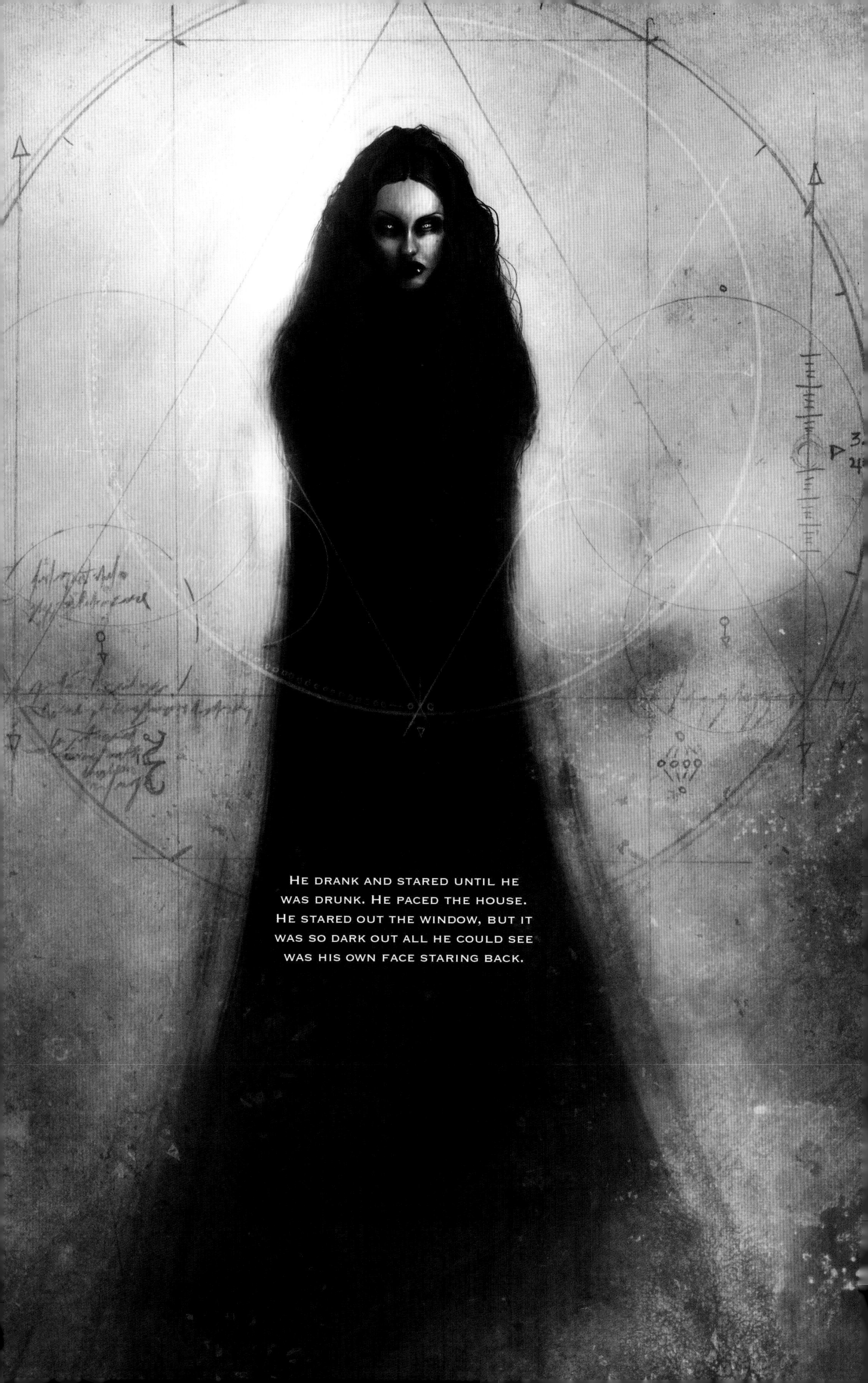
He drank and stared until he was drunk. He paced the house. He stared out the window, but it was so dark out all he could see was his own face staring back.

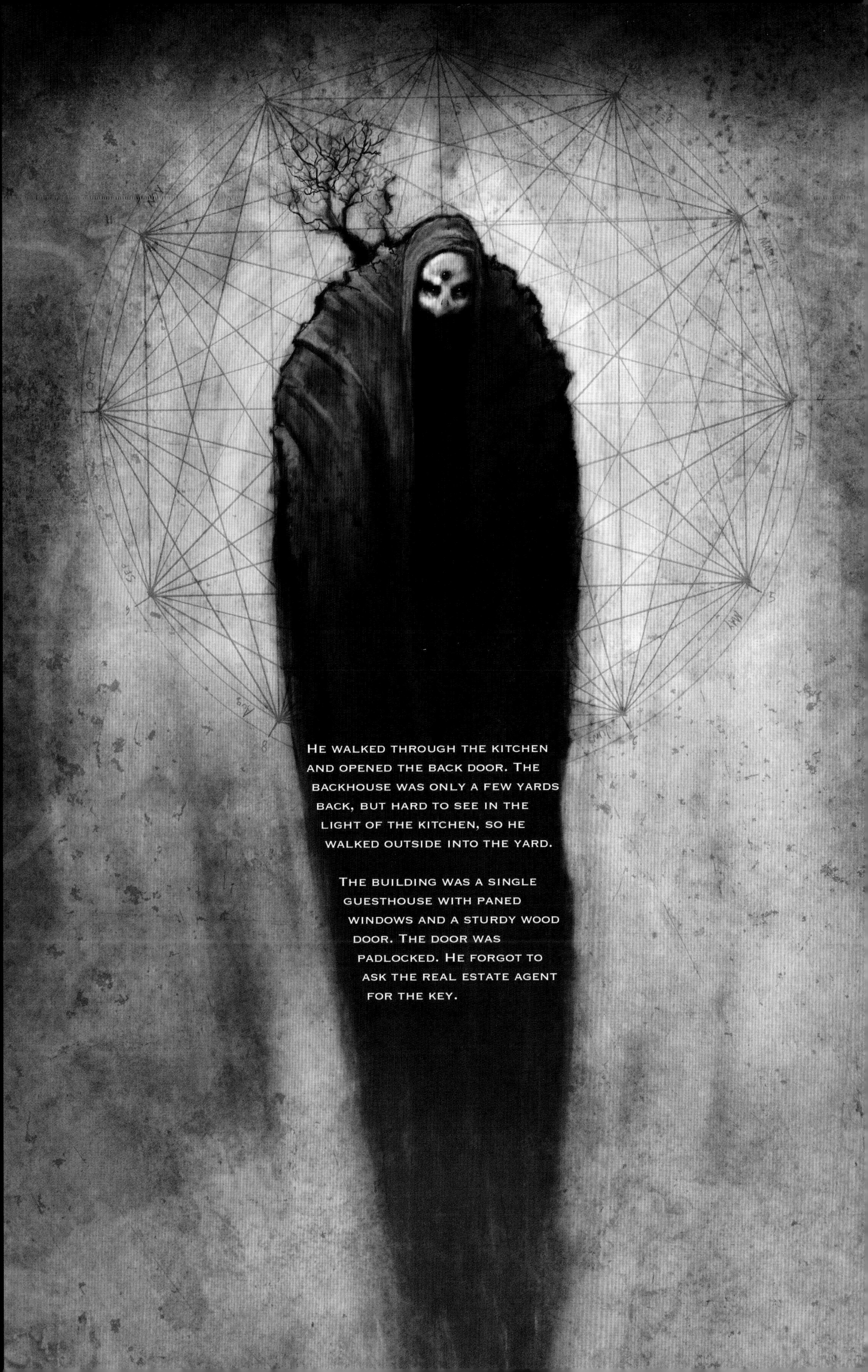

He walked through the kitchen and opened the back door. The backhouse was only a few yards back, but hard to see in the light of the kitchen, so he walked outside into the yard.

The building was a single guesthouse with paned windows and a sturdy wood door. The door was padlocked. He forgot to ask the real estate agent for the key.

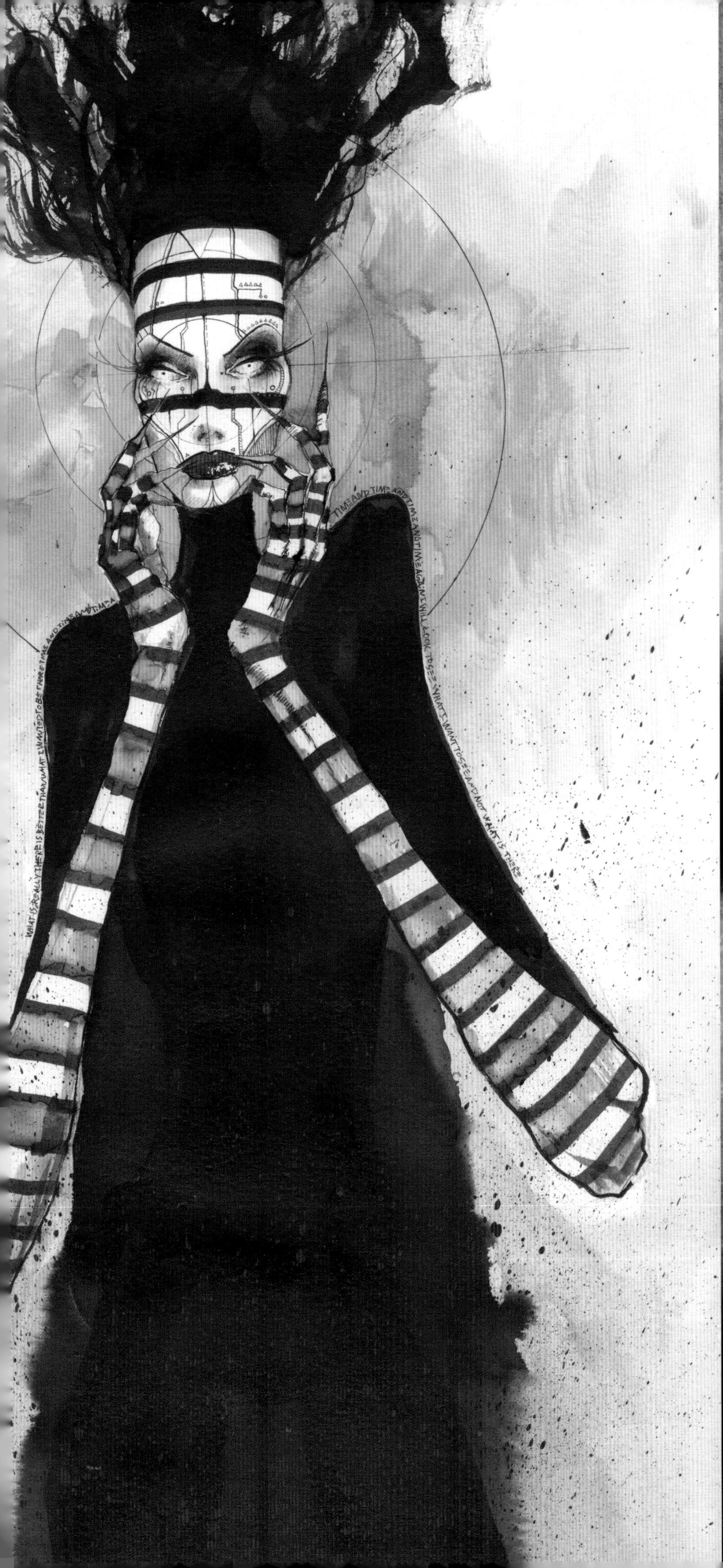
TIME AND TIME AND TIME AND TIME AGAIN I WILL LOOK TO SEE WHAT I WANT TO SEE AND NOT WHAT IS THERE
WHAT IS REALLY THERE IS BETTER THAN WHAT I WANTED TO BE THERE TIME AND TIME AND TIME A

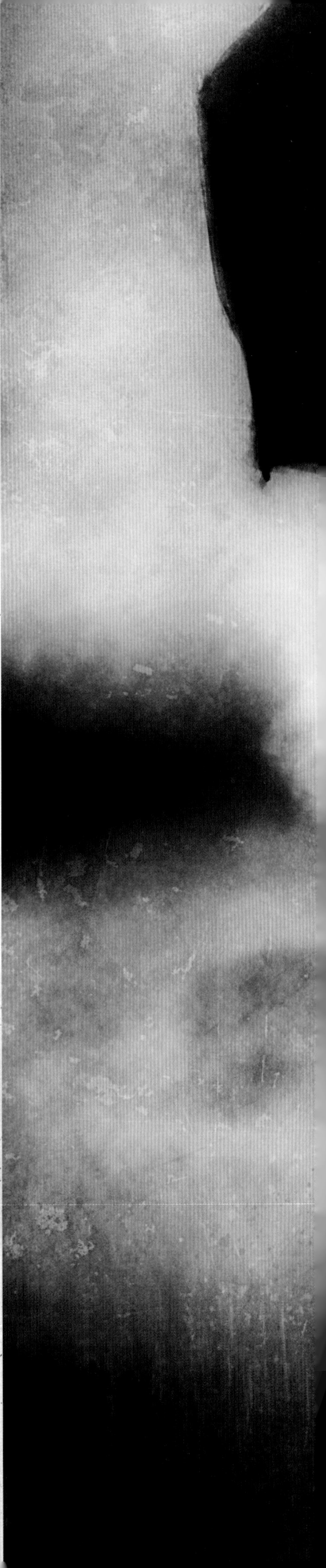

He cupped his hands and peered in through the windows but could only see a dusty floor and cobwebs. He stepped back and saw what he thought was his reflection. But it wasn't. A woman stood inside, staring back at him.

Dan stumbled back. He turned to see if anybody was in the yard with him, maybe it was his or her reflection. But when he looked back, she was still there.

She was a young woman. She wore a dusty, old-fashioned dress. Her face was pale, with sickly, white hair. She was beautiful. She drew him in.

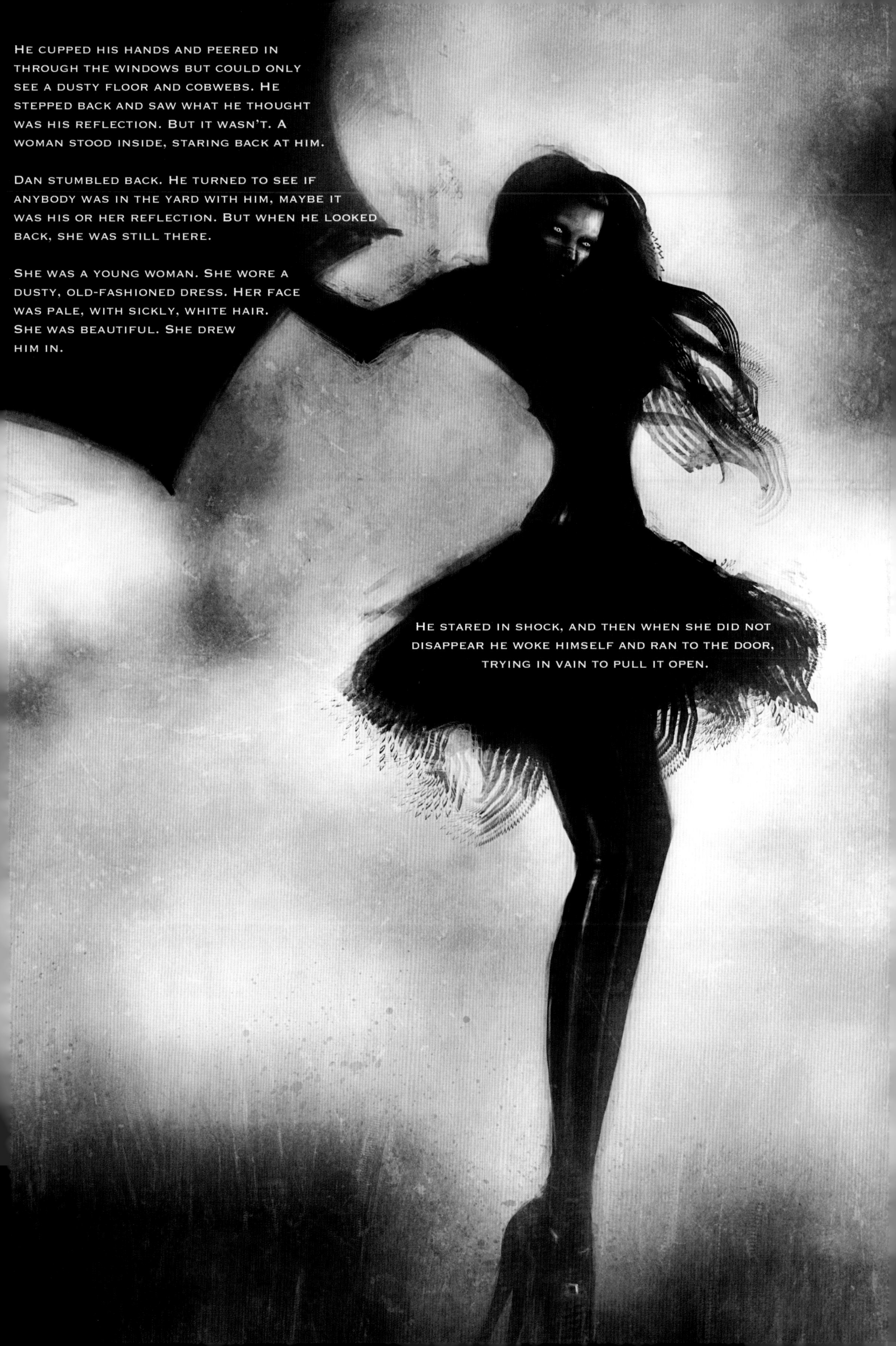

He stared in shock, and then when she did not disappear he woke himself and ran to the door, trying in vain to pull it open.

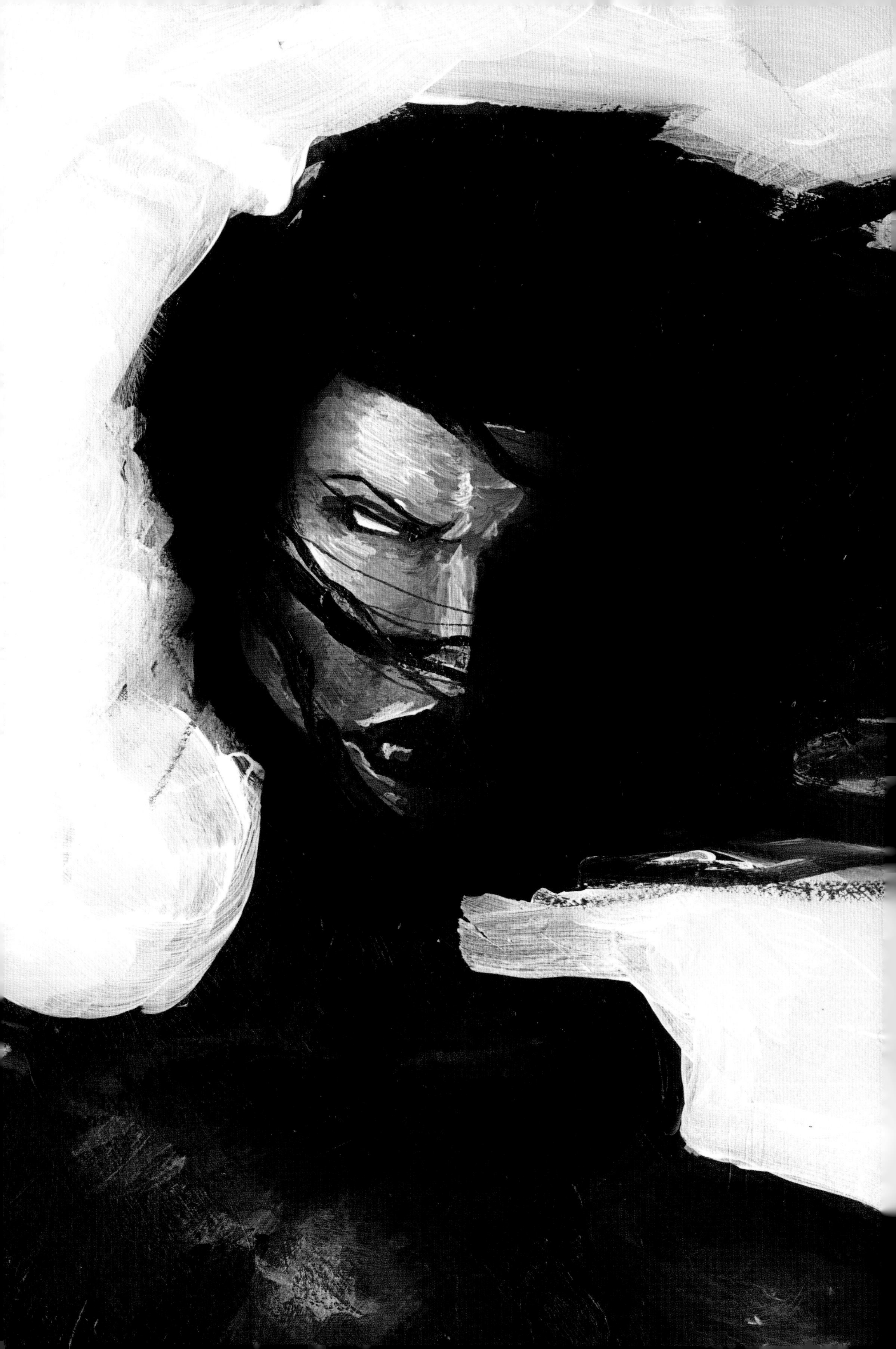

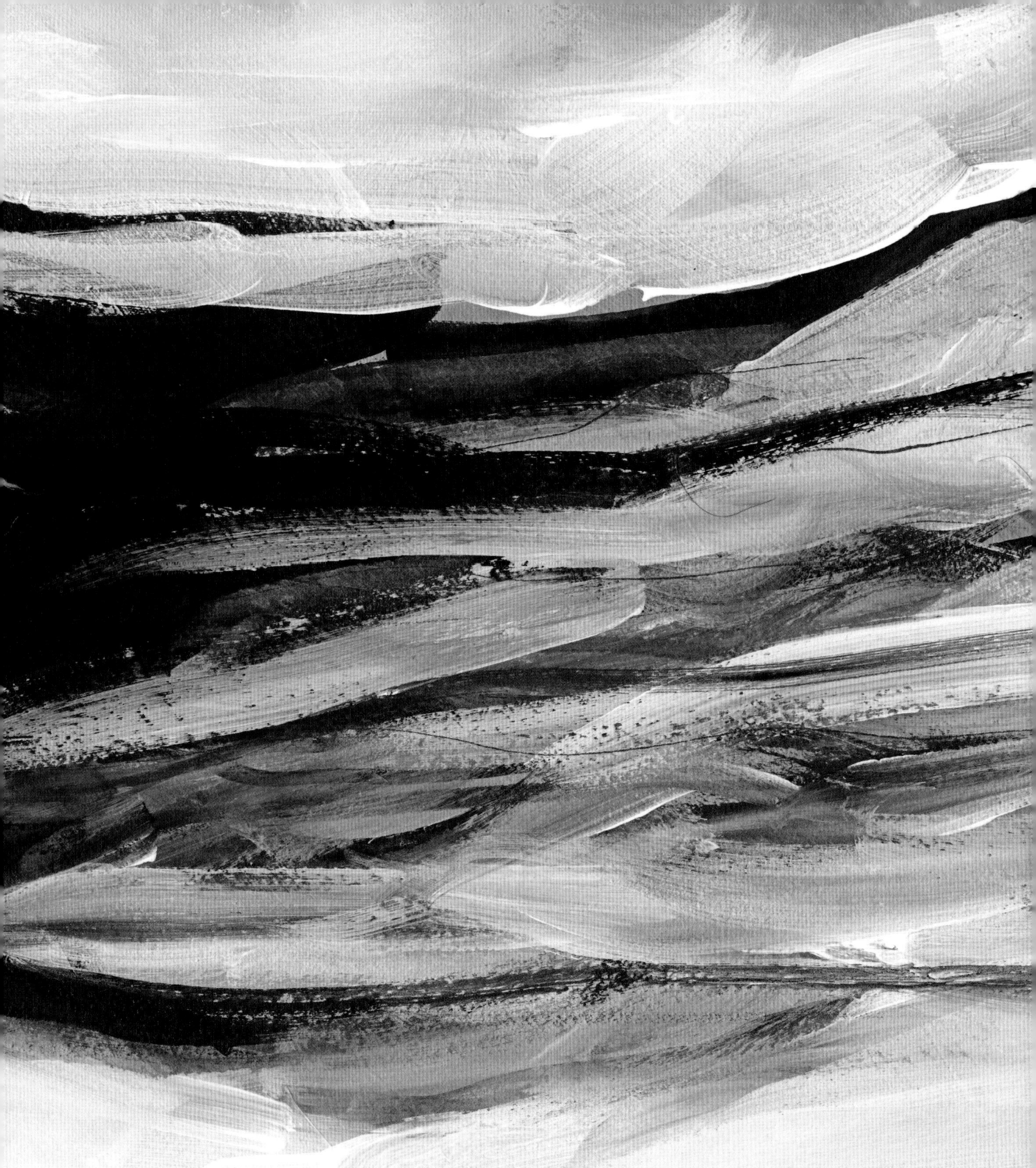

He ran to the window. She stood there, just in the moonlight.

"Stay there," he yelled. "I'll break the windows."

"No."

Her voice was all around him as she spoke.

"It's safer in here tonight," she said.

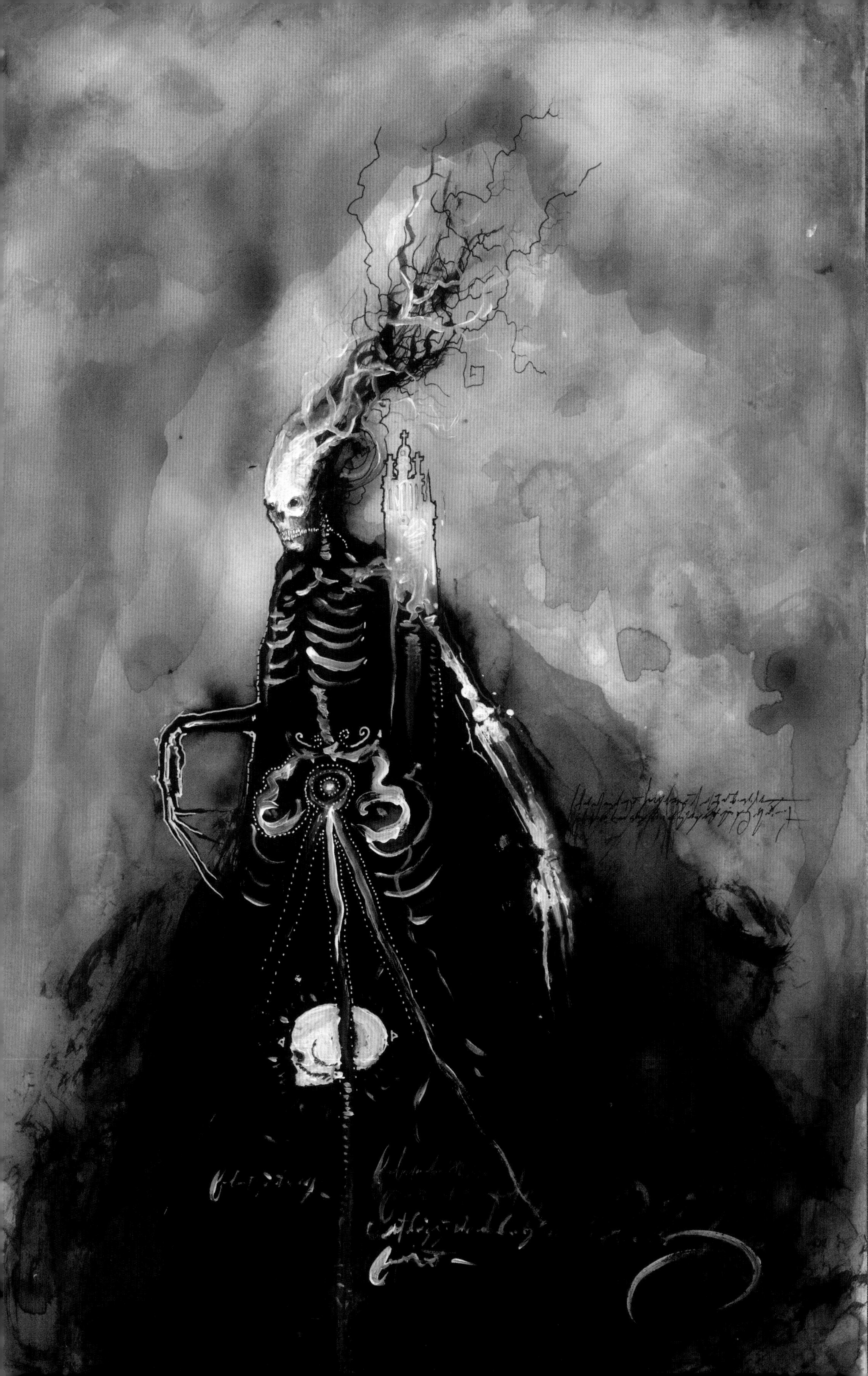

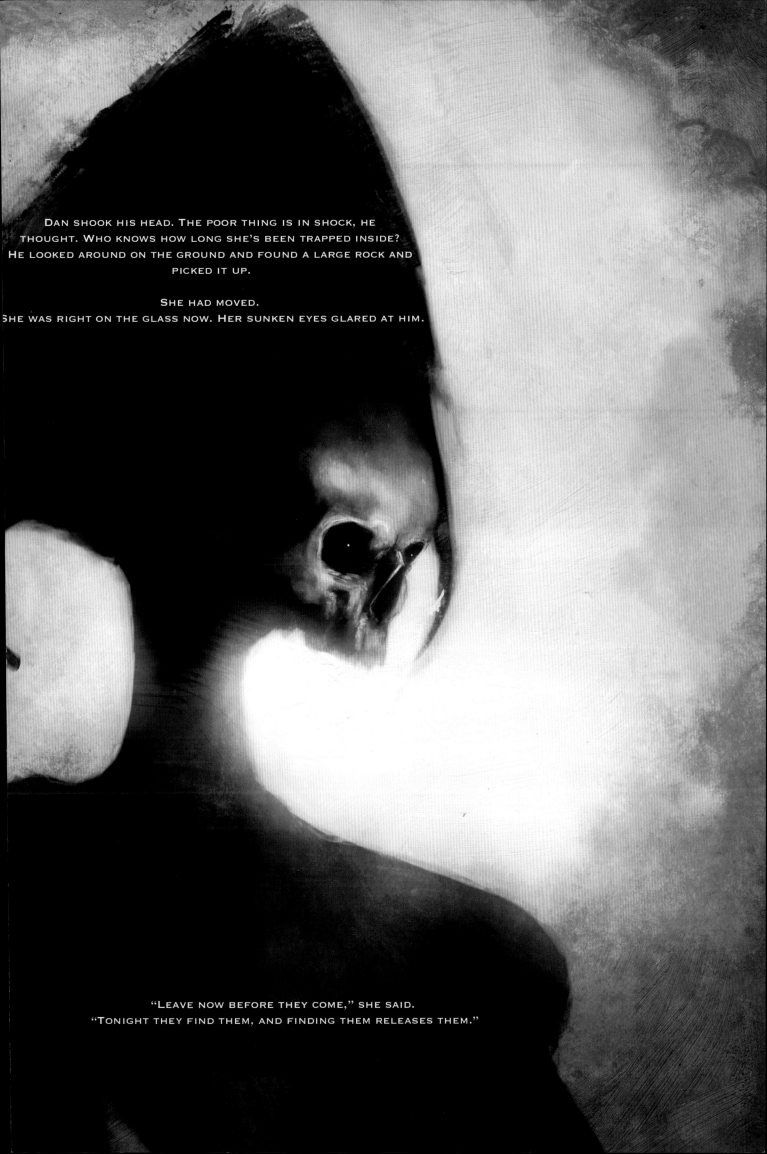

DAN SHOOK HIS HEAD. THE POOR THING IS IN SHOCK, HE
THOUGHT. WHO KNOWS HOW LONG SHE'S BEEN TRAPPED INSIDE?
HE LOOKED AROUND ON THE GROUND AND FOUND A LARGE ROCK AND
PICKED IT UP.

SHE HAD MOVED.
SHE WAS RIGHT ON THE GLASS NOW. HER SUNKEN EYES GLARED AT HIM.

"LEAVE NOW BEFORE THEY COME," SHE SAID.
"TONIGHT THEY FIND THEM, AND FINDING THEM RELEASES THEM."

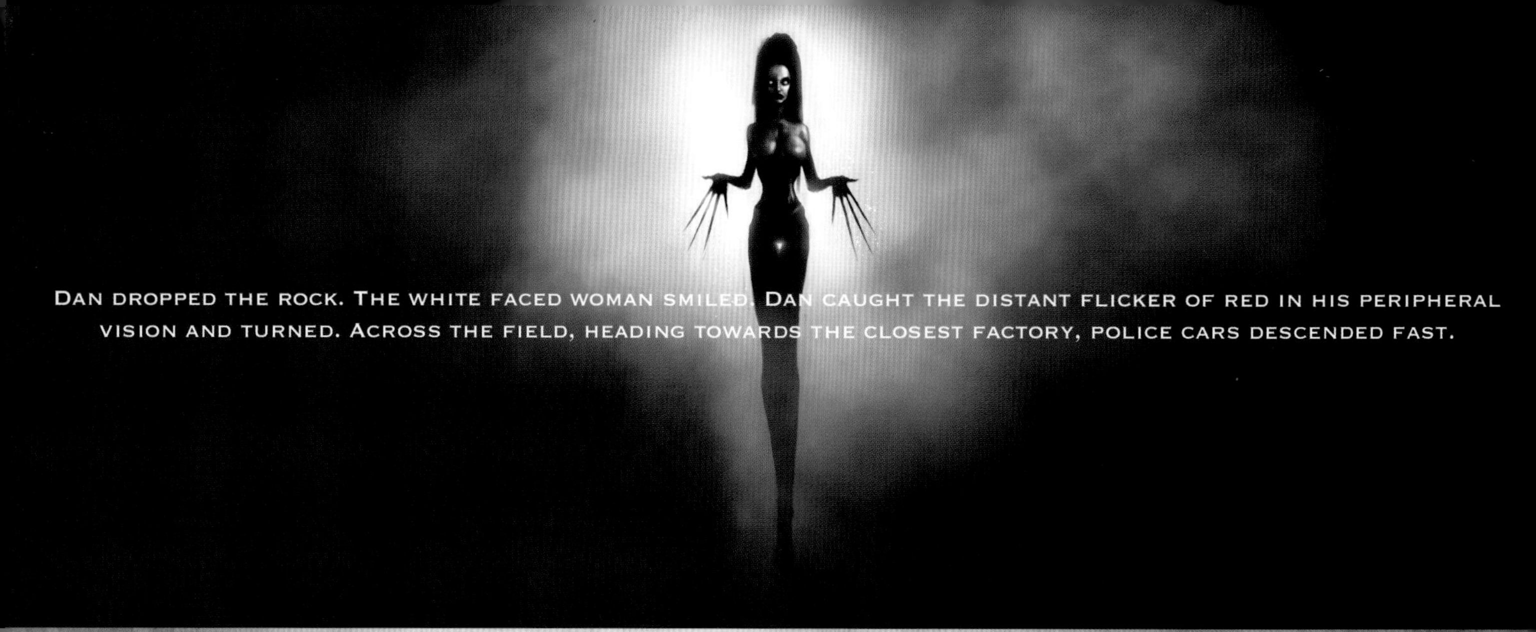
Dan dropped the rock. The white faced woman smiled. Dan caught the distant flicker of red in his peripheral vision and turned. Across the field, heading towards the closest factory, police cars descended fast.

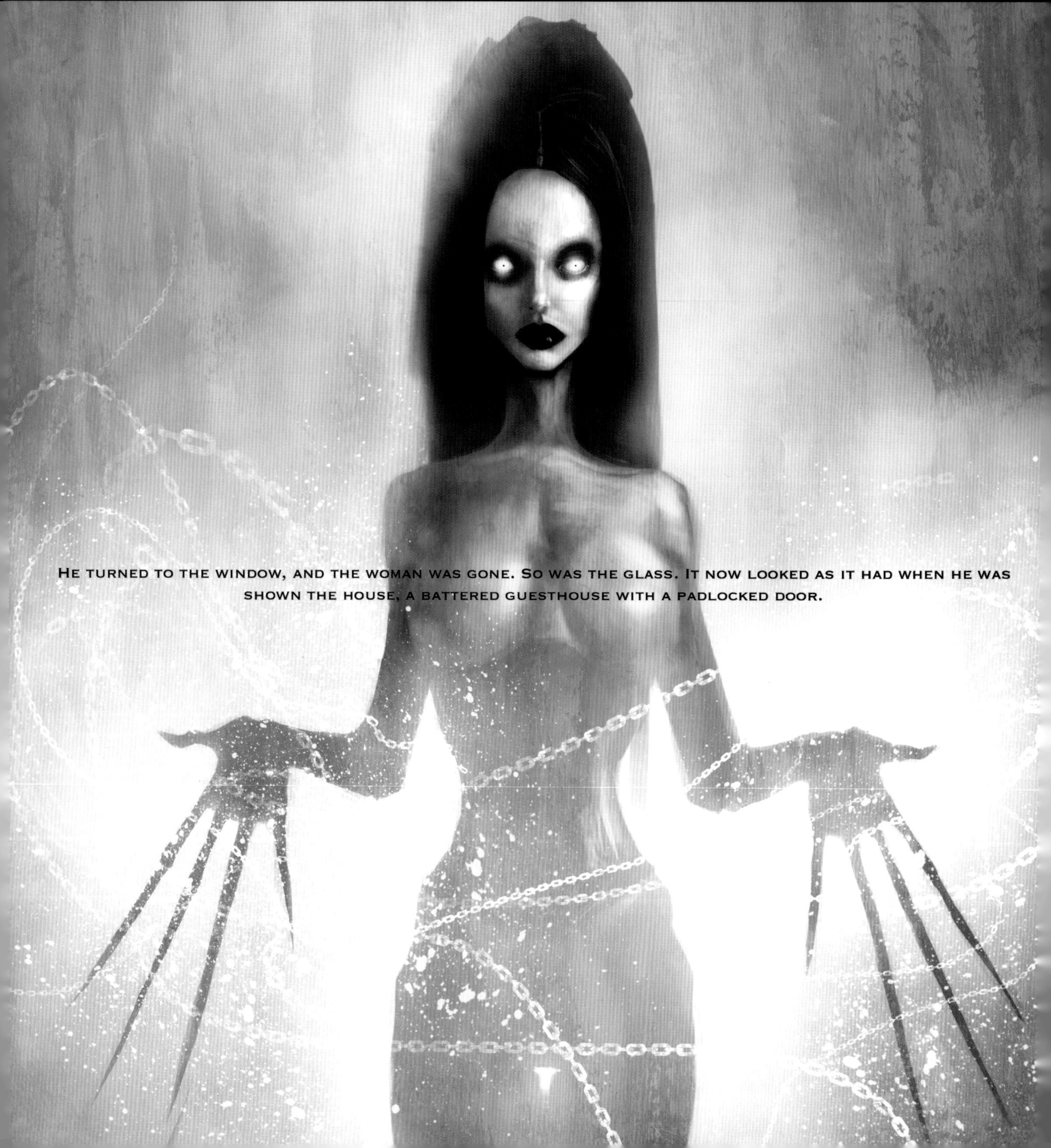
He turned to the window, and the woman was gone. So was the glass. It now looked as it had when he was shown the house, a battered guesthouse with a padlocked door.

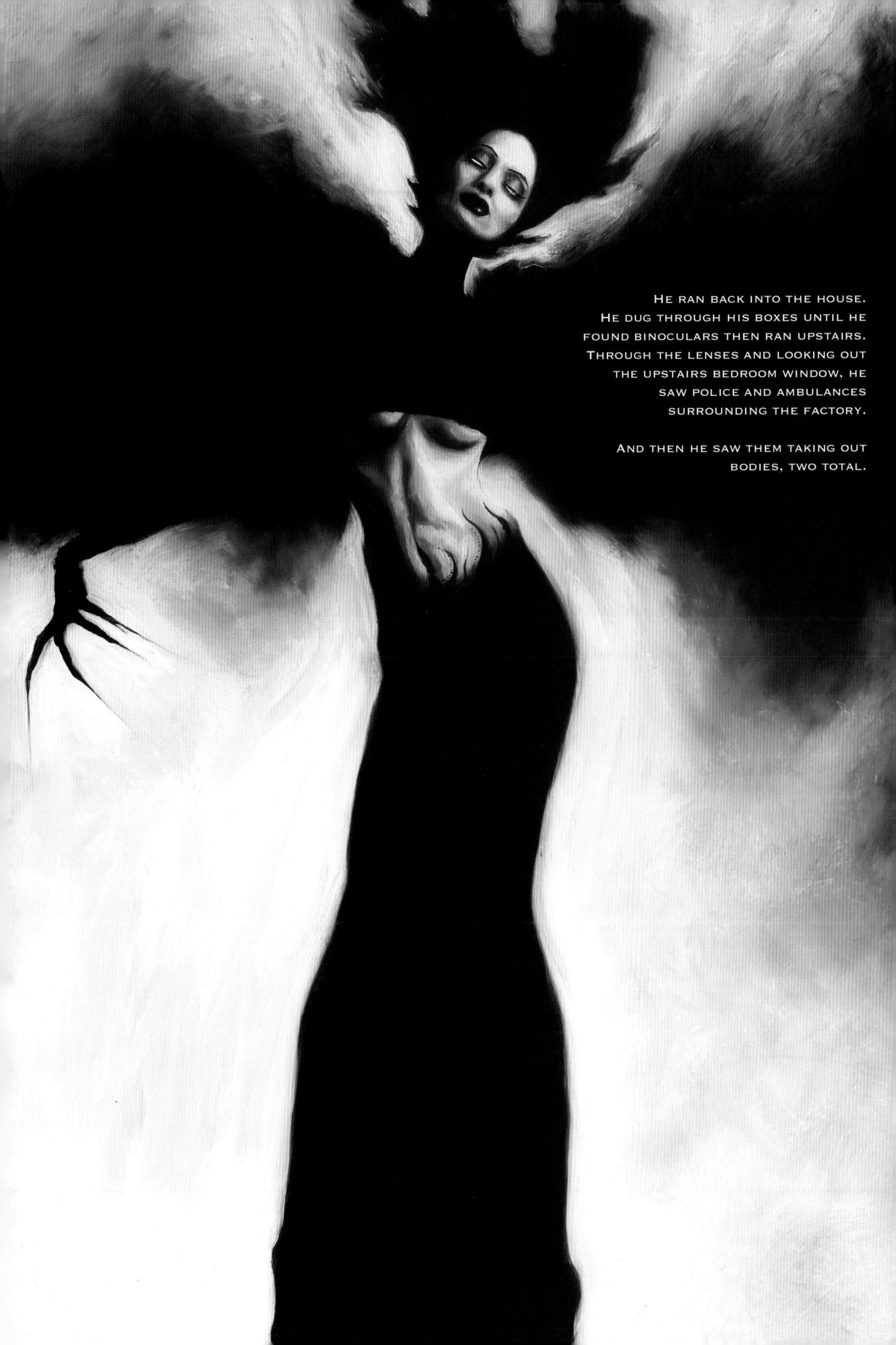
He ran back into the house.
He dug through his boxes until he
found binoculars then ran upstairs.
Through the lenses and looking out
the upstairs bedroom window, he
saw police and ambulances
surrounding the factory.

And then he saw them taking out
bodies, two total.

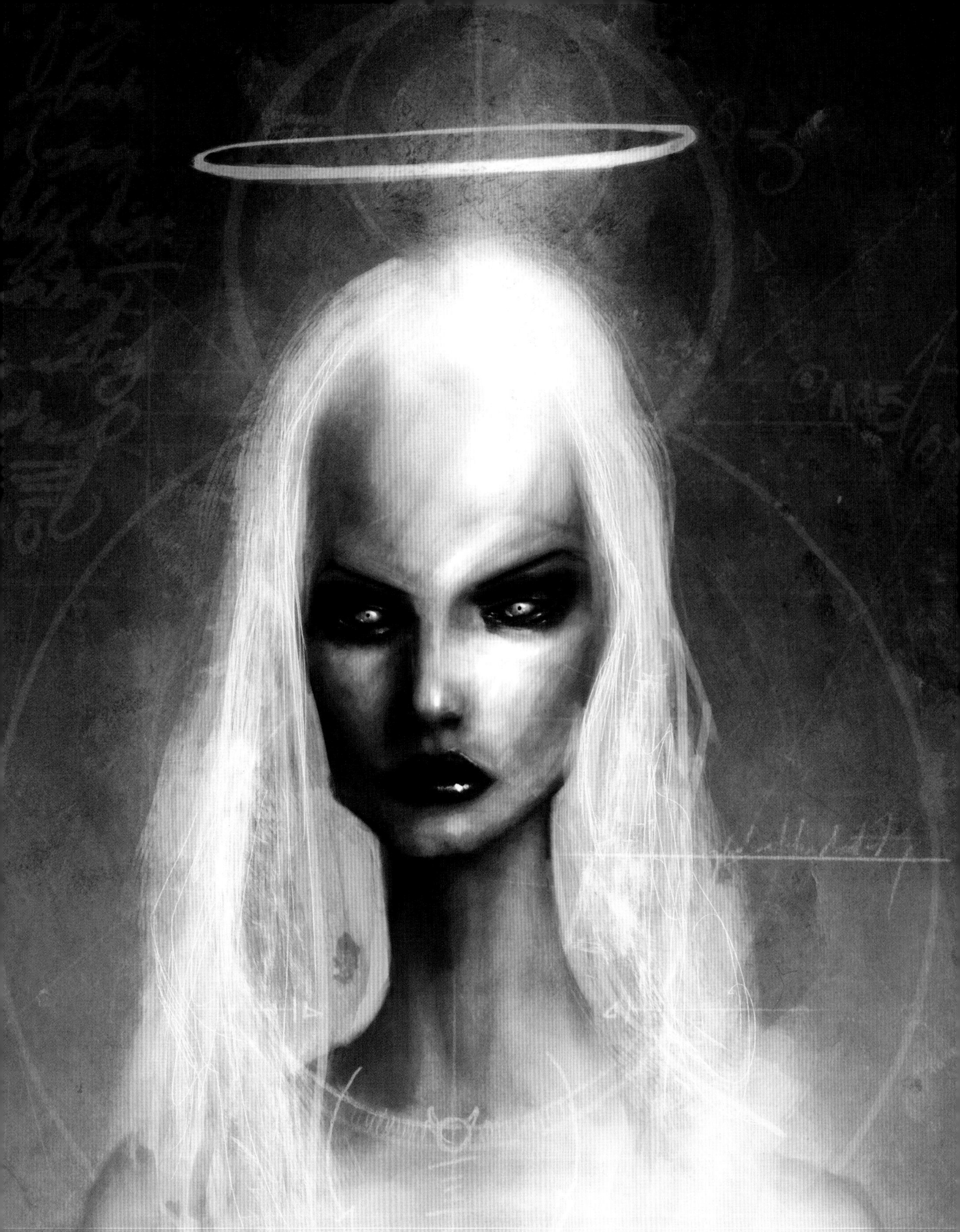

He didn't need his binoculars to see what caught his eye next, people in the field, coming towards the house. There were dozens of them.

He ran downstairs, reaching the living room as a tall woman, white-faced, and wrapped in a cloak floated into the house. Others followed, walking, plodding inside. He ran for the back door, but they were coming in there, as well.

A young woman in a pale blue dress, her belly slit open, hovered above the tiles and looked the painter in the eye.

Before he could say anything, ask who they were or what they wanted, she was on him. She attacked him and seduced him at once. She raked his flesh with her nails and kissed him softly afterwards.

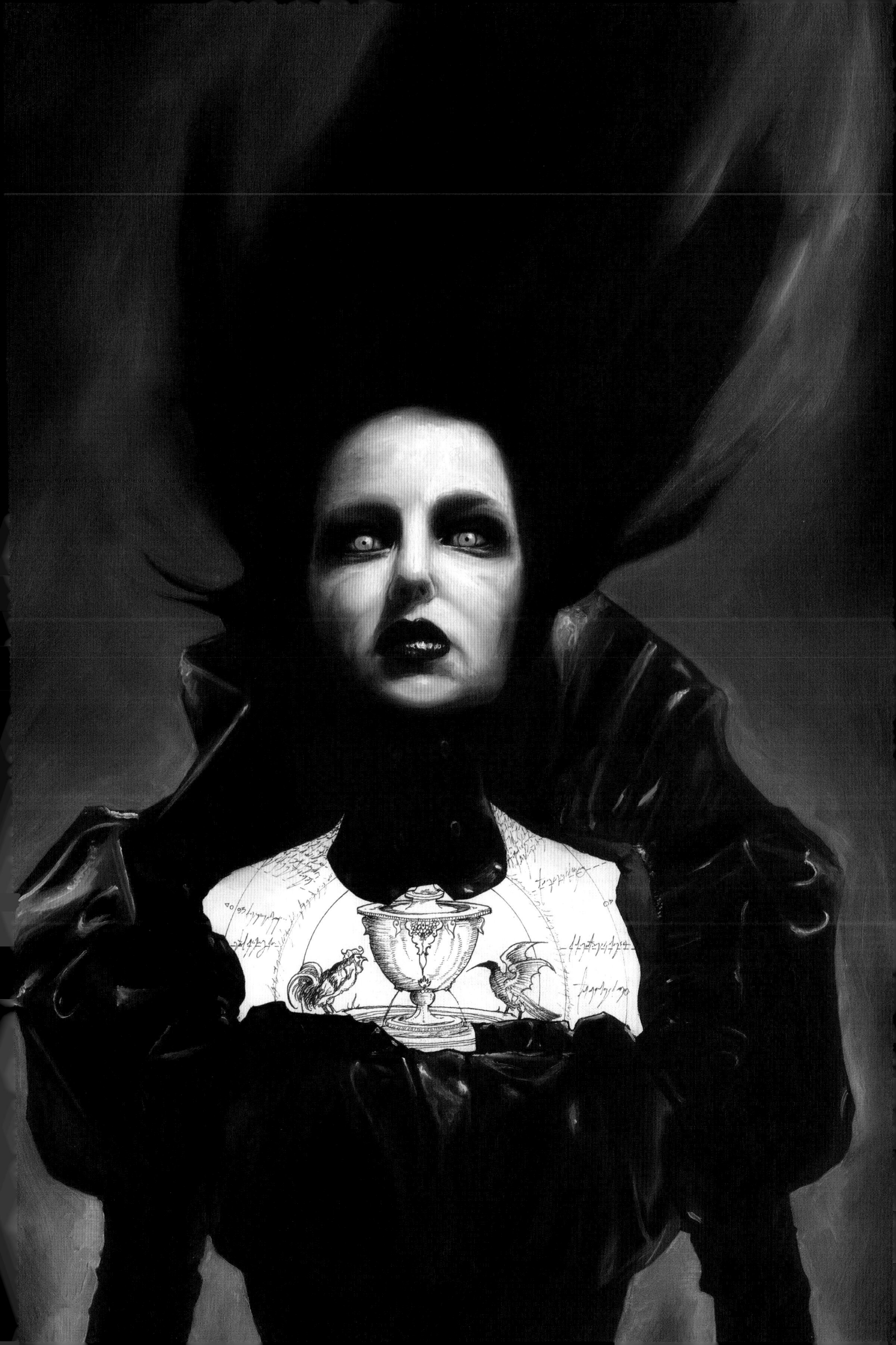

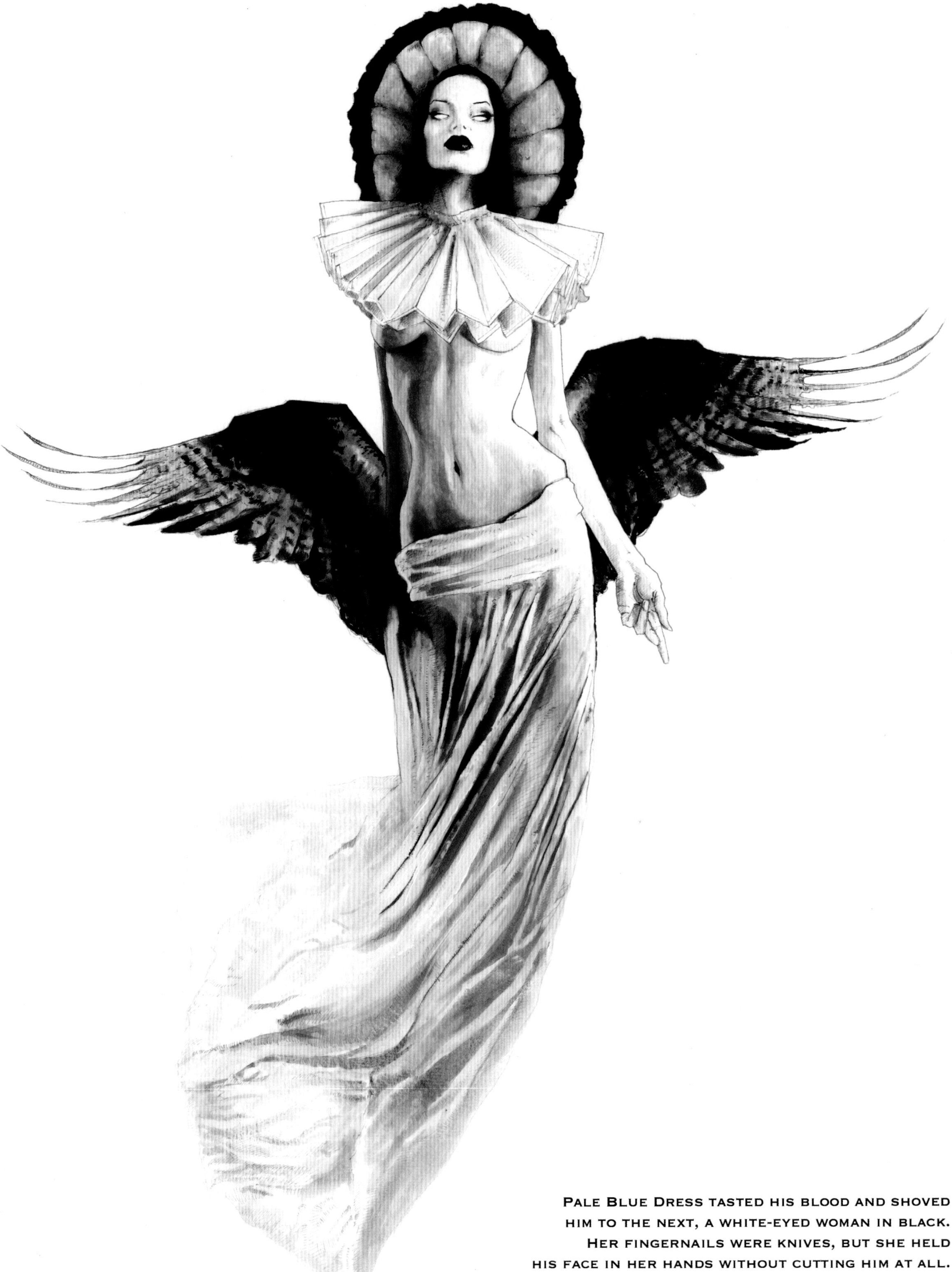

Pale Blue Dress tasted his blood and shoved
him to the next, a white-eyed woman in black.
Her fingernails were knives, but she held
his face in her hands without cutting him at all.

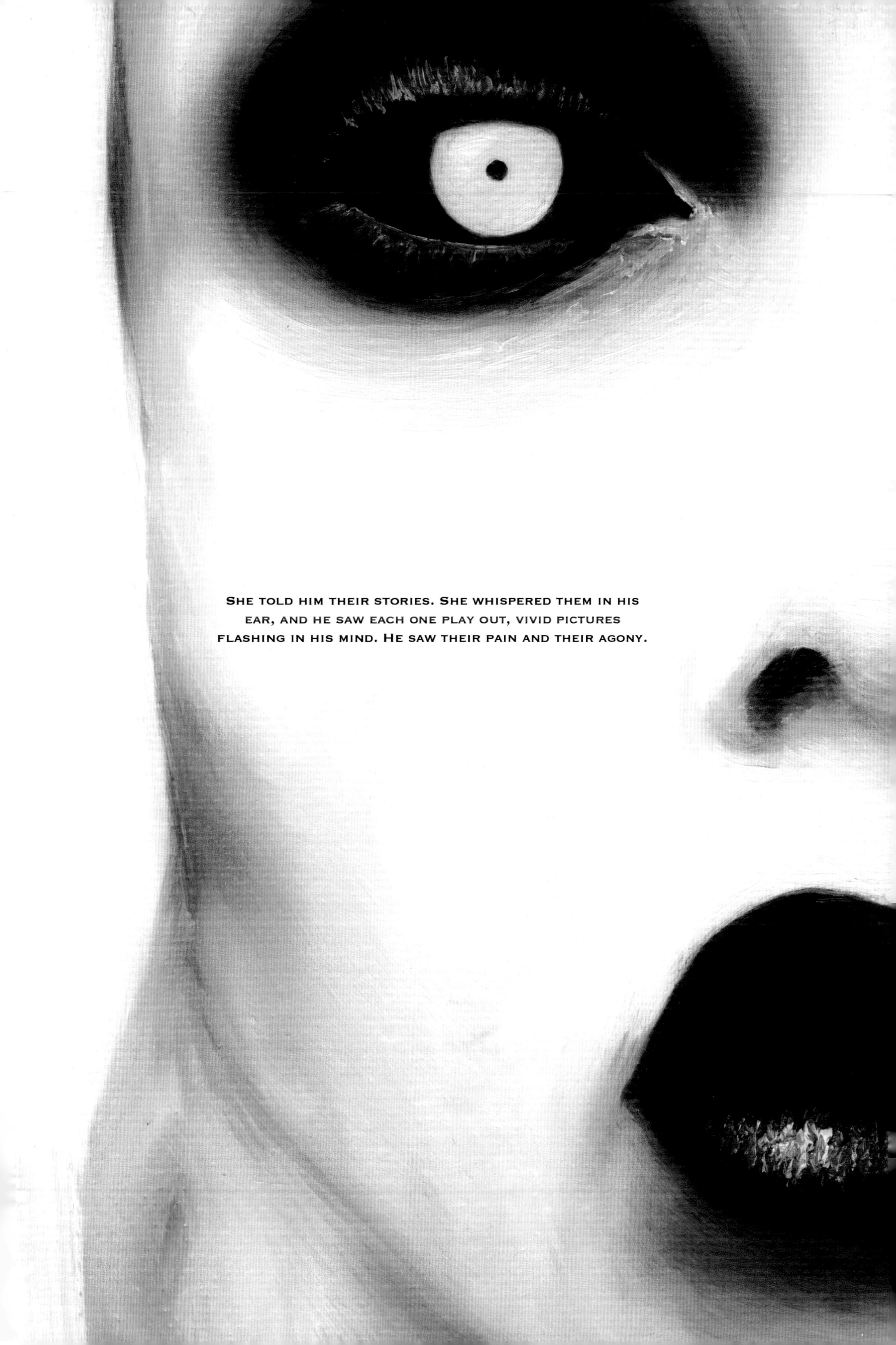

She told him their stories. She whispered them in his ear, and he saw each one play out, vivid pictures flashing in his mind. He saw their pain and their agony.

HE SAW ALL THEIR DREAMS DASHED BY SUDDEN VIOLENCE AND GREED. HE SAW SOMETHING BEAUTIFUL DESTROYED OVER AND OVER AND OVER. ALL WERE DIFFERENT AND SO MUCH THE SAME, DREAMS DASHED BECAUSE OF ANOTHER'S DREAM. NEVER SATISFIED. THE MORE THEY TOOK, THE MORE THEY NEEDED.

THE HOUSE FILLED WITH THE DEAD TRAVELING FROM ONE TRAGEDY TO THE NEXT, PICKING UP NEW MEMBERS AS IT ROLLED ENDLESSLY ON.

AND NOW THEY HAD SOMEONE TO TELL THEIR STORIES TO, AND THEY TOLD THEM UNTIL DAN FELL ON THE FLOOR QUIVERING IN A BALL OF SWEAT.

HE WAITED FOR THE DEATHBLOW THAT NEVER CAME. ONCE THEY WERE DONE WITH HIM, THEY LEFT AS THEY HAD COME. HE OPENED HIS EYES TO AN EMPTY HOUSE.

THEY LEFT SOMETHING FOR HIM.

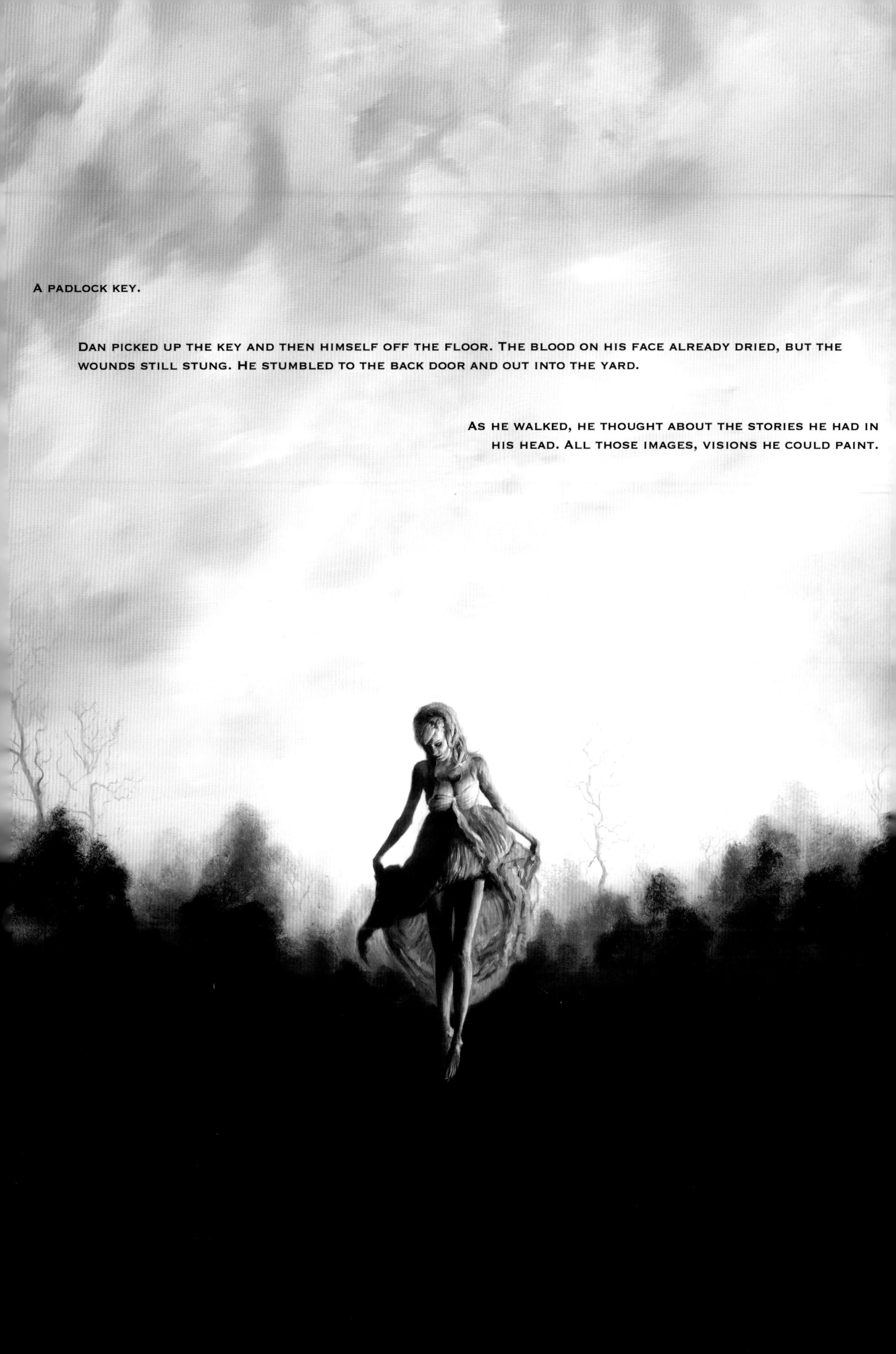
A padlock key.
Dan picked up the key and then himself off the floor. The blood on his face already dried, but the wounds still stung. He stumbled to the back door and out into the yard.
As he walked, he thought about the stories he had in his head. All those images, visions he could paint.

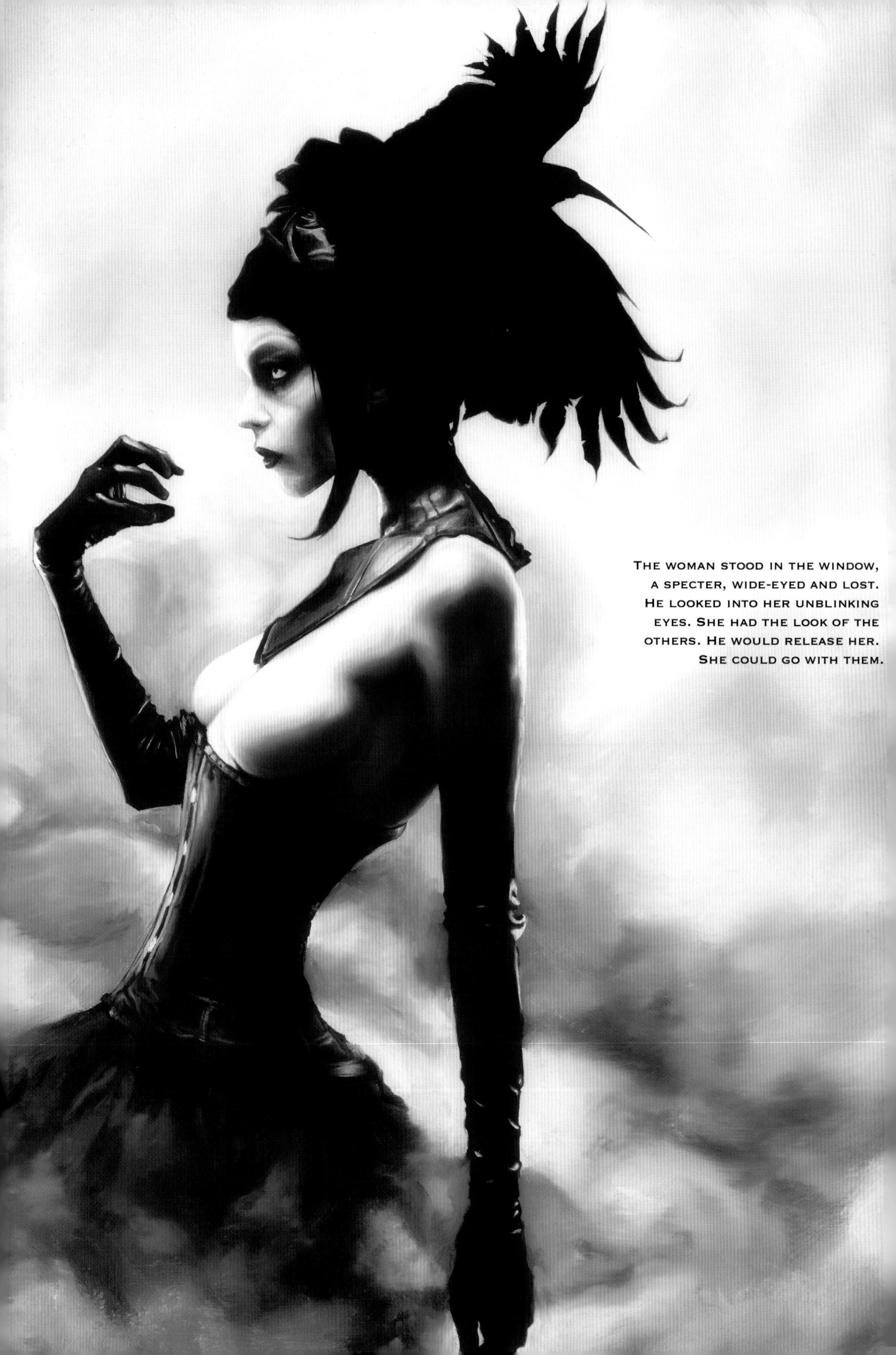

The woman stood in the window, a specter, wide-eyed and lost. He looked into her unblinking eyes. She had the look of the others. He would release her. She could go with them.

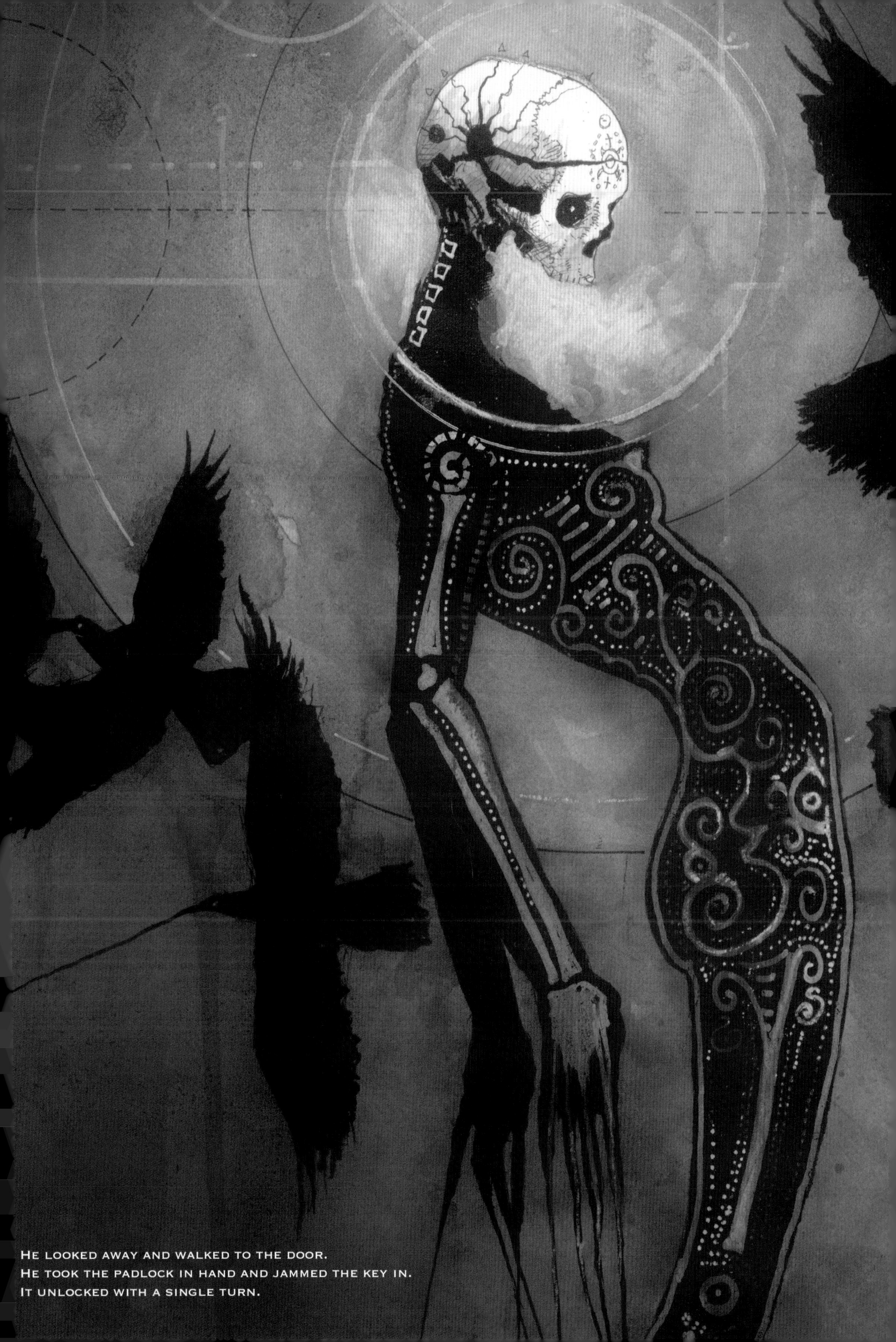

He looked away and walked to the door.
He took the padlock in hand and jammed the key in.
It unlocked with a single turn.

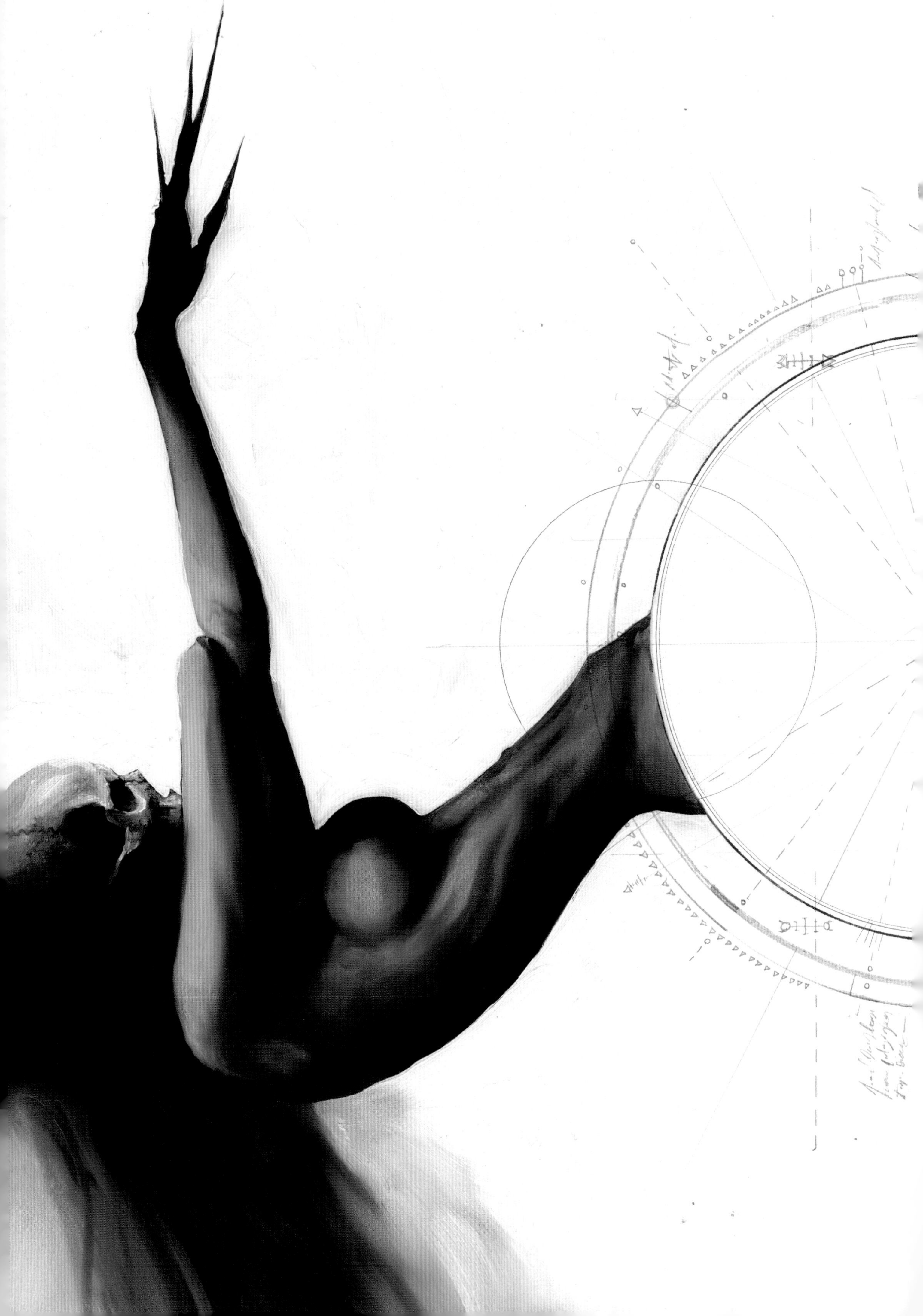

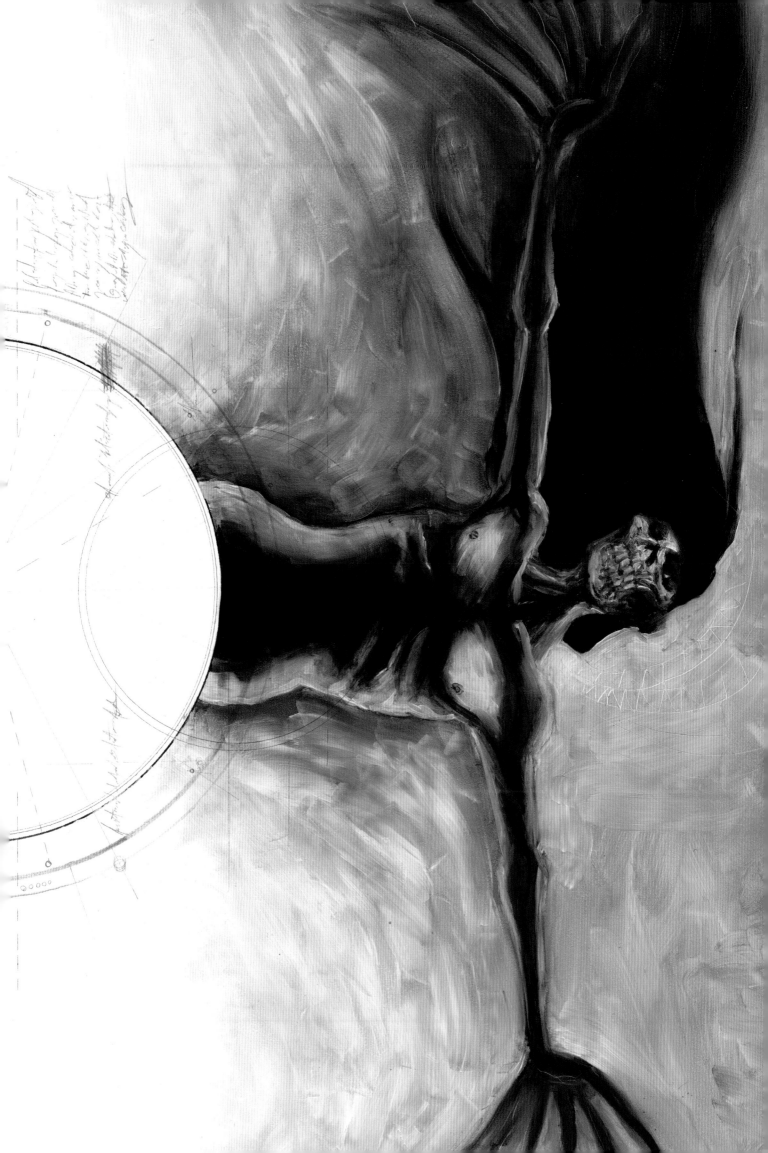

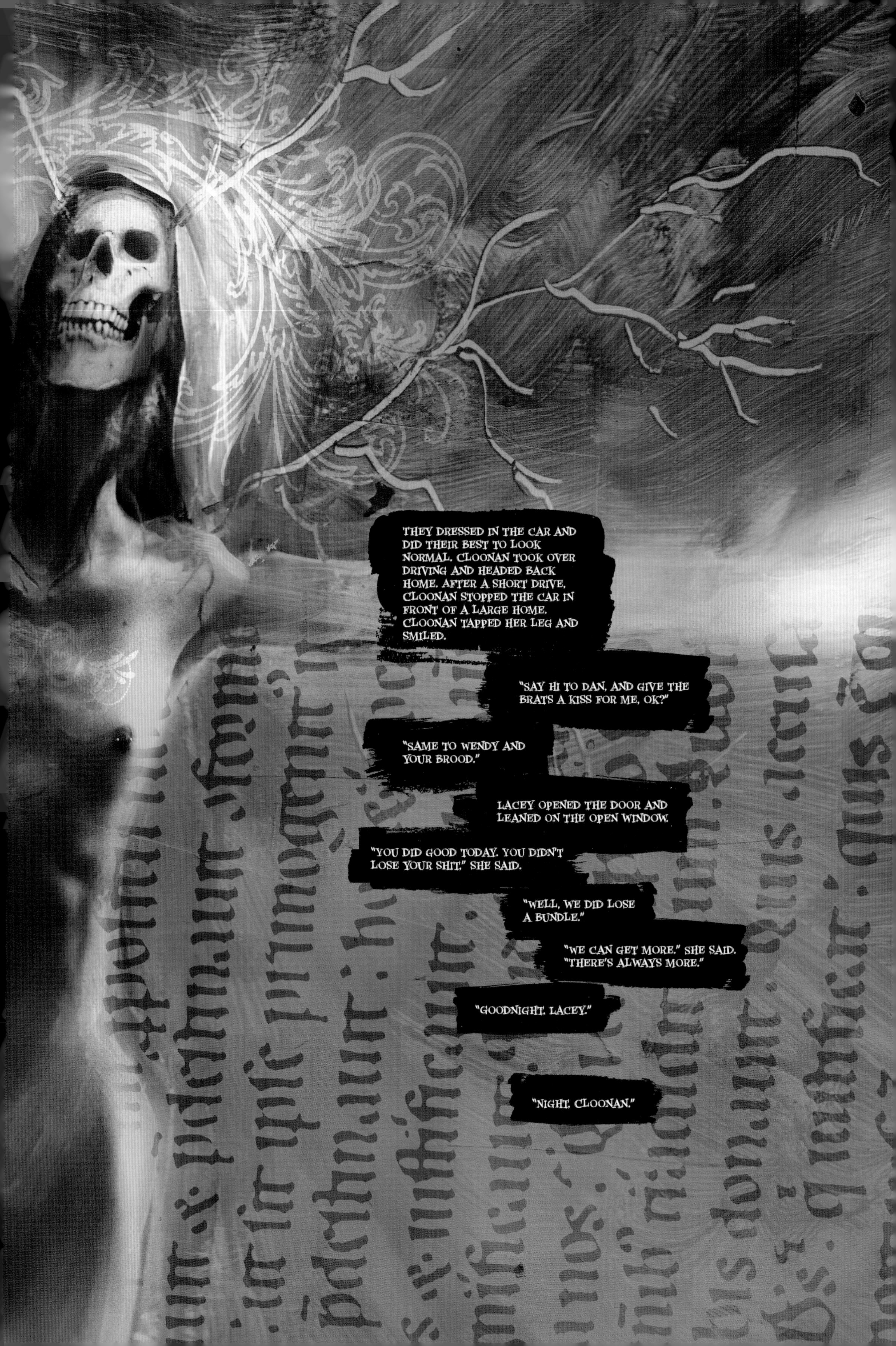
THEY DRESSED IN THE CAR AND DID THEIR BEST TO LOOK NORMAL. CLOONAN TOOK OVER DRIVING AND HEADED BACK HOME. AFTER A SHORT DRIVE, CLOONAN STOPPED THE CAR IN FRONT OF A LARGE HOME. CLOONAN TAPPED HER LEG AND SMILED.
"SAY HI TO DAN, AND GIVE THE BRATS A KISS FOR ME, OK?"
"SAME TO WENDY AND YOUR BROOD."
LACEY OPENED THE DOOR AND LEANED ON THE OPEN WINDOW.
"YOU DID GOOD TODAY. YOU DIDN'T LOSE YOUR SHIT," SHE SAID.
"WELL, WE DID LOSE A BUNDLE."
"WE CAN GET MORE," SHE SAID. "THERE'S ALWAYS MORE."
"GOODNIGHT, LACEY."
"NIGHT, CLOONAN."

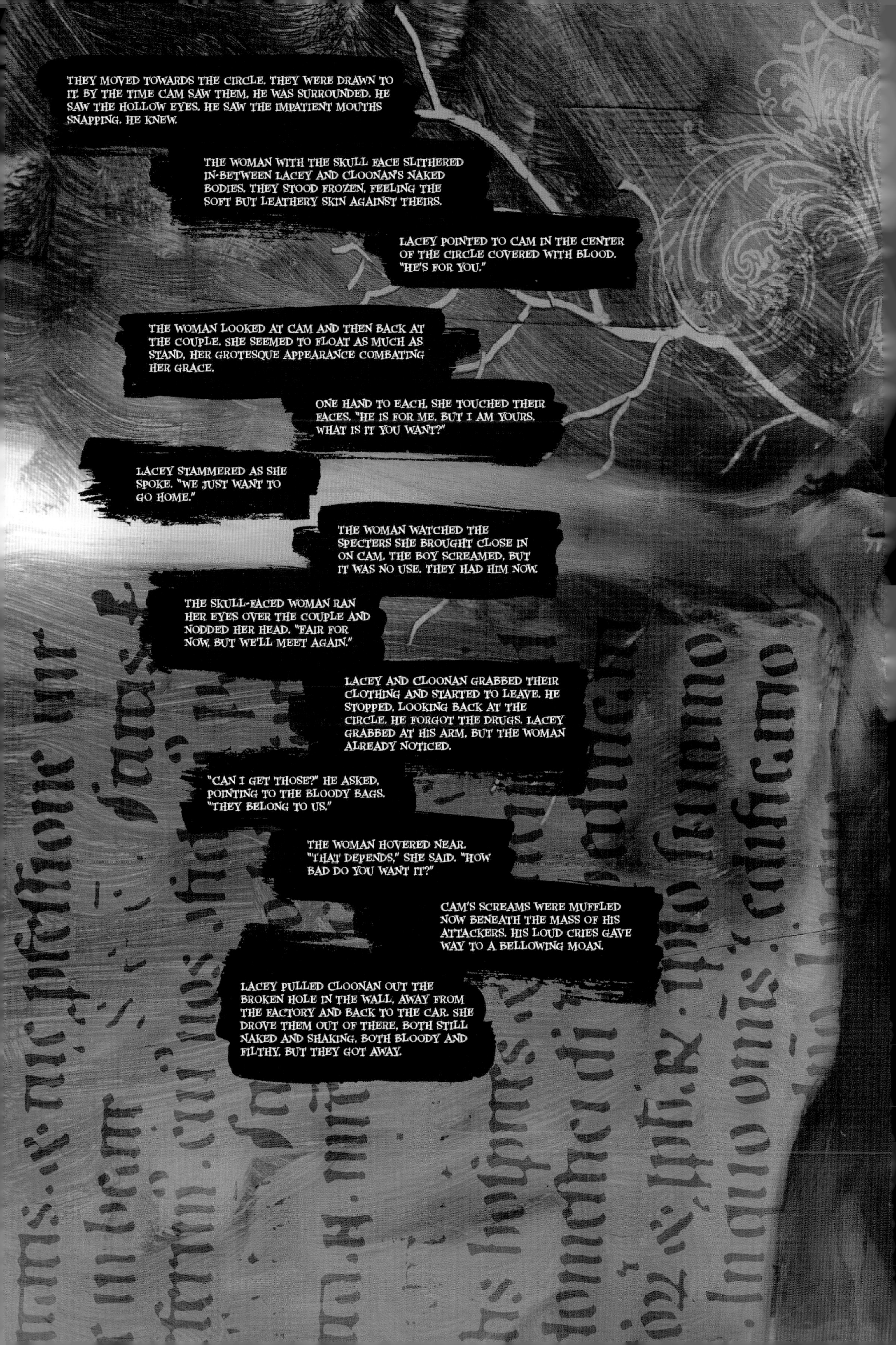
THEY MOVED TOWARDS THE CIRCLE. THEY WERE DRAWN TO IT. BY THE TIME CAM SAW THEM, HE WAS SURROUNDED. HE SAW THE HOLLOW EYES. HE SAW THE IMPATIENT MOUTHS SNAPPING. HE KNEW.
THE WOMAN WITH THE SKULL FACE SLITHERED IN-BETWEEN LACEY AND CLOONAN'S NAKED BODIES. THEY STOOD FROZEN, FEELING THE SOFT BUT LEATHERY SKIN AGAINST THEIRS.
LACEY POINTED TO CAM IN THE CENTER OF THE CIRCLE COVERED WITH BLOOD. "HE'S FOR YOU."
THE WOMAN LOOKED AT CAM AND THEN BACK AT THE COUPLE. SHE SEEMED TO FLOAT AS MUCH AS STAND, HER GROTESQUE APPEARANCE COMBATING HER GRACE.
ONE HAND TO EACH, SHE TOUCHED THEIR FACES. "HE IS FOR ME, BUT I AM YOURS. WHAT IS IT YOU WANT?"
LACEY STAMMERED AS SHE SPOKE. "WE JUST WANT TO GO HOME."
THE WOMAN WATCHED THE SPECTERS SHE BROUGHT CLOSE IN ON CAM. THE BOY SCREAMED, BUT IT WAS NO USE. THEY HAD HIM NOW.
THE SKULL-FACED WOMAN RAN HER EYES OVER THE COUPLE AND NODDED HER HEAD. "FAIR FOR NOW, BUT WE'LL MEET AGAIN."
LACEY AND CLOONAN GRABBED THEIR CLOTHING AND STARTED TO LEAVE. HE STOPPED, LOOKING BACK AT THE CIRCLE. HE FORGOT THE DRUGS. LACEY GRABBED AT HIS ARM, BUT THE WOMAN ALREADY NOTICED.
"CAN I GET THOSE?" HE ASKED, POINTING TO THE BLOODY BAGS. "THEY BELONG TO US."
THE WOMAN HOVERED NEAR. "THAT DEPENDS," SHE SAID. "HOW BAD DO YOU WANT IT?"
CAM'S SCREAMS WERE MUFFLED NOW BENEATH THE MASS OF HIS ATTACKERS. HIS LOUD CRIES GAVE WAY TO A BELLOWING MOAN.
LACEY PULLED CLOONAN OUT THE BROKEN HOLE IN THE WALL, AWAY FROM THE FACTORY AND BACK TO THE CAR. SHE DROVE THEM OUT OF THERE, BOTH STILL NAKED AND SHAKING, BOTH BLOODY AND FILTHY, BUT THEY GOT AWAY.

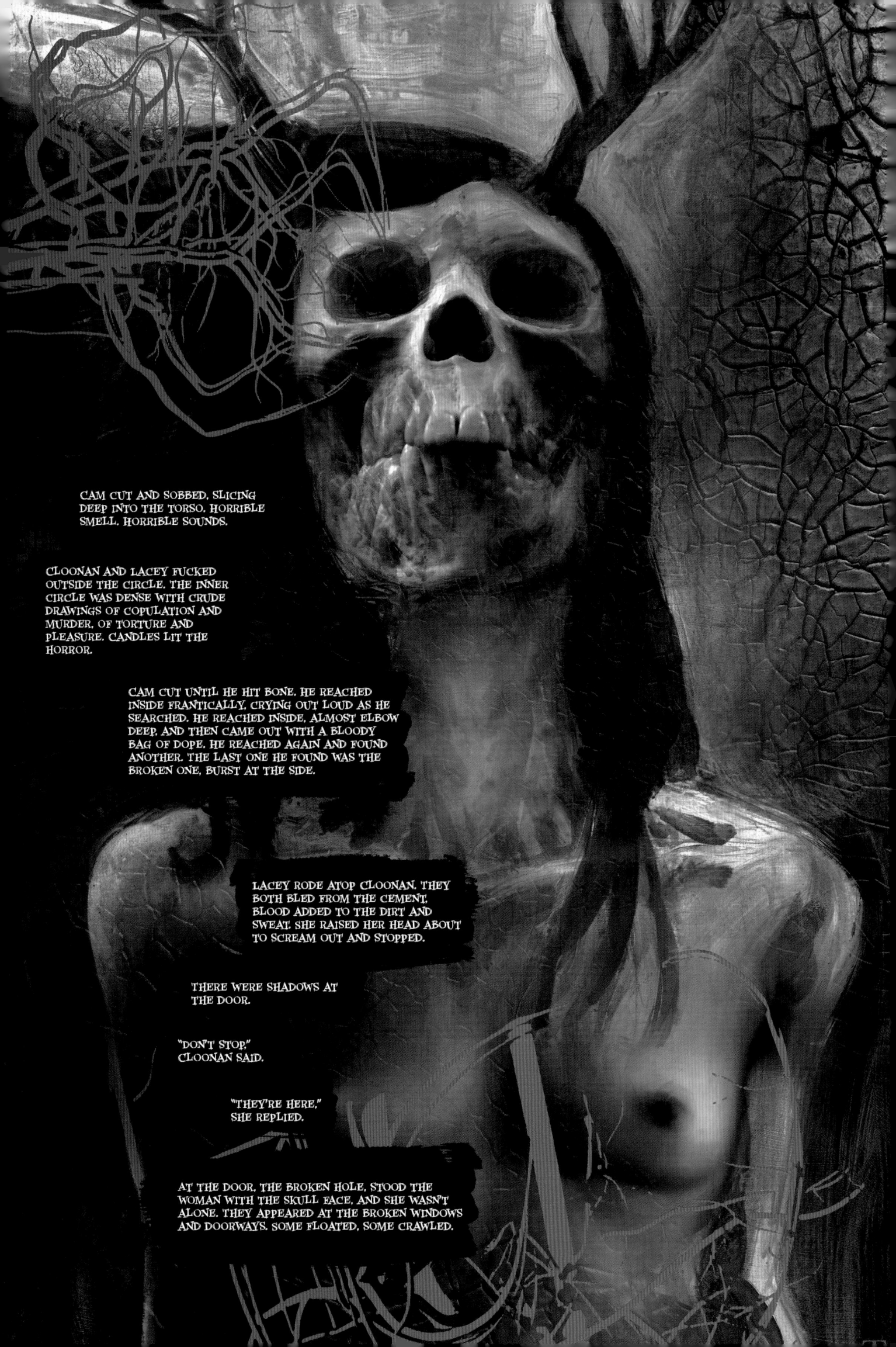

CAM CUT AND SOBBED, SLICING
DEEP INTO THE TORSO. HORRIBLE
SMELL. HORRIBLE SOUNDS.

CLOONAN AND LACEY FUCKED
OUTSIDE THE CIRCLE. THE INNER
CIRCLE WAS DENSE WITH CRUDE
DRAWINGS OF COPULATION AND
MURDER, OF TORTURE AND
PLEASURE. CANDLES LIT THE
HORROR.

CAM CUT UNTIL HE HIT BONE. HE REACHED
INSIDE FRANTICALLY, CRYING OUT LOUD AS HE
SEARCHED. HE REACHED INSIDE, ALMOST ELBOW
DEEP, AND THEN CAME OUT WITH A BLOODY
BAG OF DOPE. HE REACHED AGAIN AND FOUND
ANOTHER. THE LAST ONE HE FOUND WAS THE
BROKEN ONE, BURST AT THE SIDE.

LACEY RODE ATOP CLOONAN. THEY
BOTH BLED FROM THE CEMENT,
BLOOD ADDED TO THE DIRT AND
SWEAT. SHE RAISED HER HEAD ABOUT
TO SCREAM OUT AND STOPPED.

THERE WERE SHADOWS AT
THE DOOR.

"DON'T STOP,"
CLOONAN SAID.

"THEY'RE HERE,"
SHE REPLIED.

AT THE DOOR, THE BROKEN HOLE, STOOD THE
WOMAN WITH THE SKULL FACE, AND SHE WASN'T
ALONE. THEY APPEARED AT THE BROKEN WINDOWS
AND DOORWAYS. SOME FLOATED, SOME CRAWLED.

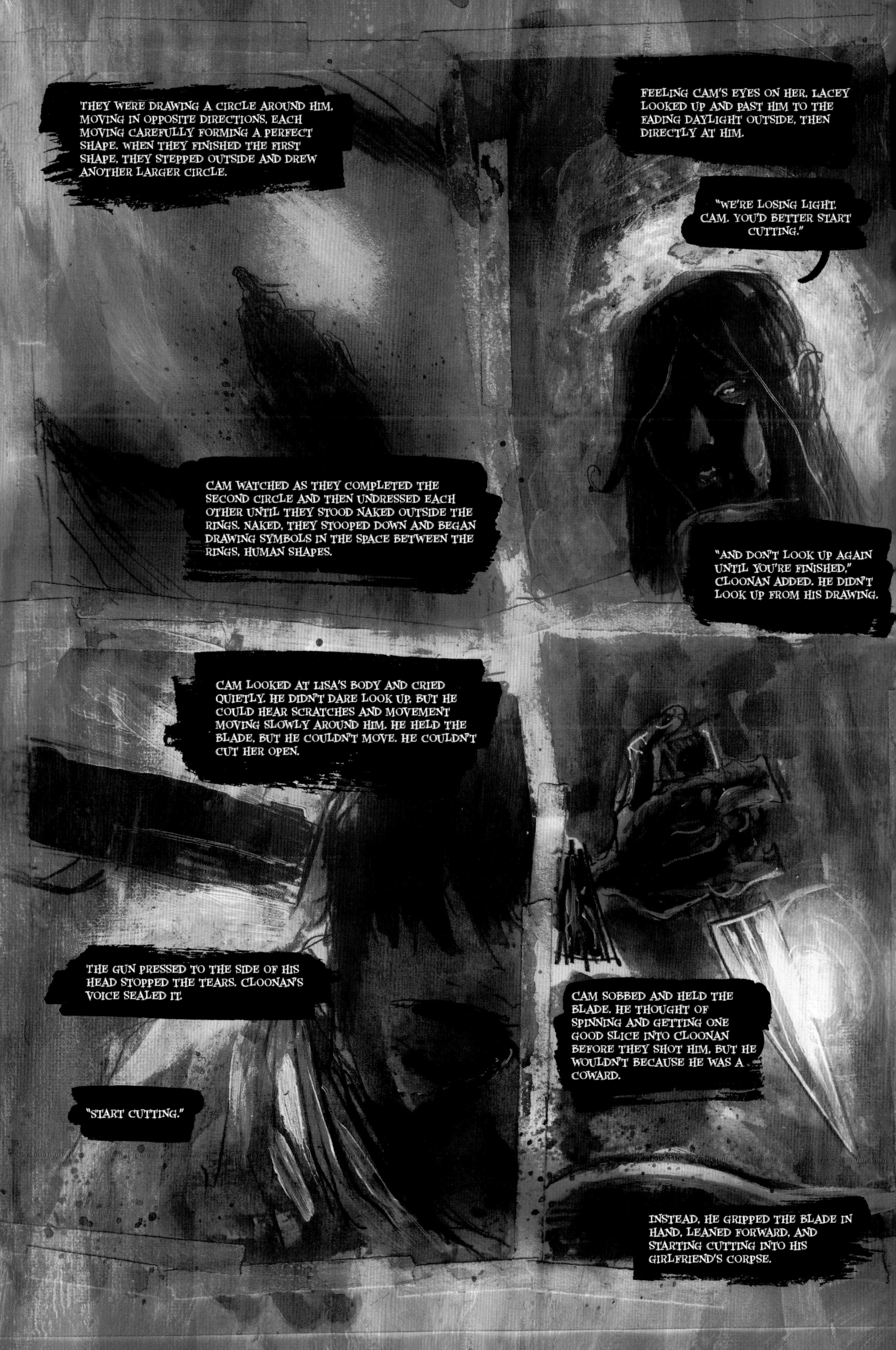
THEY WERE DRAWING A CIRCLE AROUND HIM, MOVING IN OPPOSITE DIRECTIONS, EACH MOVING CAREFULLY FORMING A PERFECT SHAPE. WHEN THEY FINISHED THE FIRST SHAPE, THEY STEPPED OUTSIDE AND DREW ANOTHER LARGER CIRCLE.
CAM WATCHED AS THEY COMPLETED THE SECOND CIRCLE AND THEN UNDRESSED EACH OTHER UNTIL THEY STOOD NAKED OUTSIDE THE RINGS. NAKED, THEY STOOPED DOWN AND BEGAN DRAWING SYMBOLS IN THE SPACE BETWEEN THE RINGS, HUMAN SHAPES.
FEELING CAM'S EYES ON HER, LACEY LOOKED UP AND PAST HIM TO THE FADING DAYLIGHT OUTSIDE, THEN DIRECTLY AT HIM.
"WE'RE LOSING LIGHT, CAM. YOU'D BETTER START CUTTING."
"AND DON'T LOOK UP AGAIN UNTIL YOU'RE FINISHED," CLOONAN ADDED. HE DIDN'T LOOK UP FROM HIS DRAWING.
CAM LOOKED AT LISA'S BODY AND CRIED QUIETLY. HE DIDN'T DARE LOOK UP, BUT HE COULD HEAR SCRATCHES AND MOVEMENT MOVING SLOWLY AROUND HIM. HE HELD THE BLADE, BUT HE COULDN'T MOVE. HE COULDN'T CUT HER OPEN.
THE GUN PRESSED TO THE SIDE OF HIS HEAD STOPPED THE TEARS. CLOONAN'S VOICE SEALED IT.
"START CUTTING."
CAM SOBBED AND HELD THE BLADE. HE THOUGHT OF SPINNING AND GETTING ONE GOOD SLICE INTO CLOONAN BEFORE THEY SHOT HIM, BUT HE WOULDN'T BECAUSE HE WAS A COWARD.
INSTEAD, HE GRIPPED THE BLADE IN HAND, LEANED FORWARD, AND STARTING CUTTING INTO HIS GIRLFRIEND'S CORPSE.

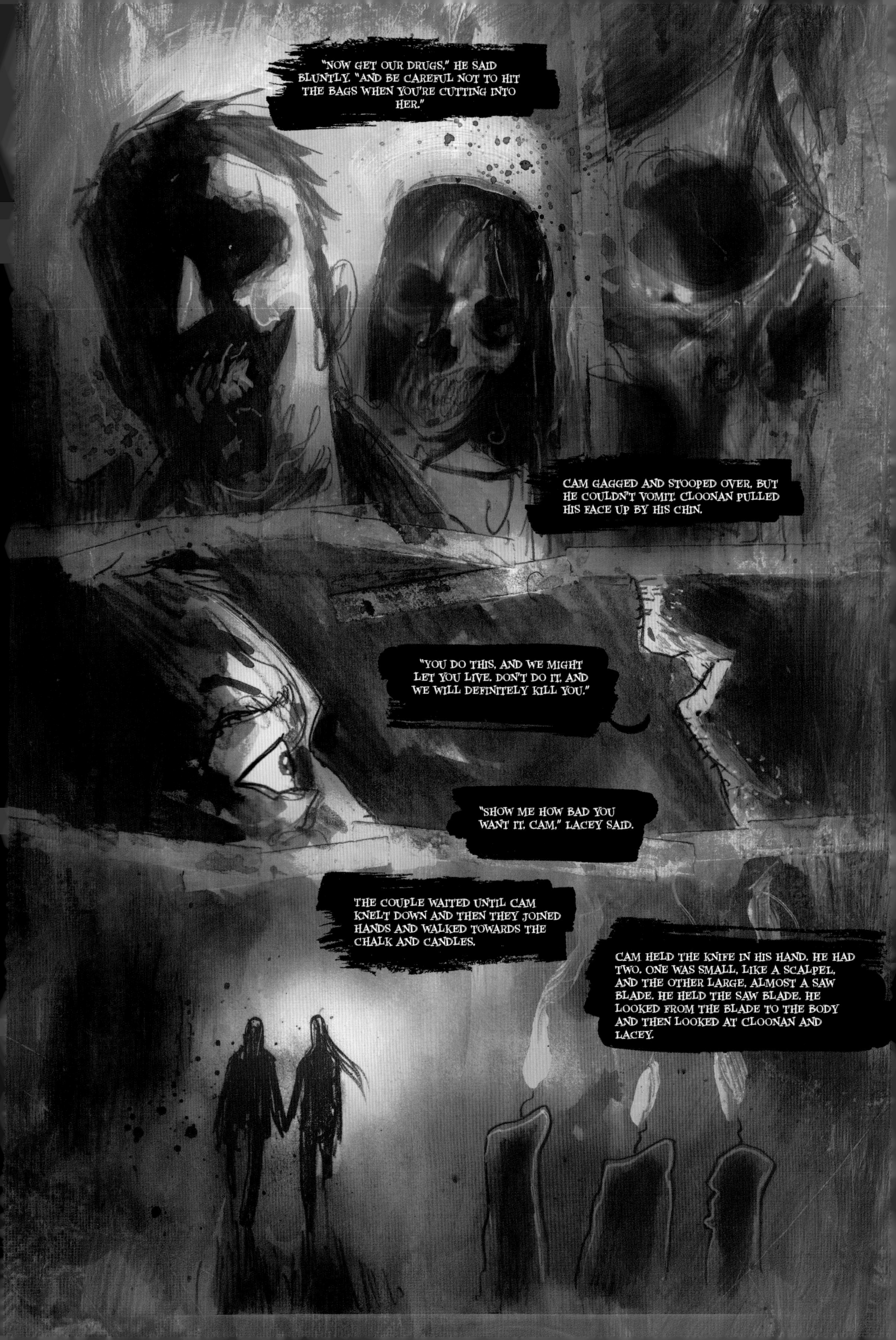
"NOW GET OUR DRUGS," HE SAID BLUNTLY. "AND BE CAREFUL NOT TO HIT THE BAGS WHEN YOU'RE CUTTING INTO HER."
CAM GAGGED AND STOOPED OVER, BUT HE COULDN'T VOMIT. CLOONAN PULLED HIS FACE UP BY HIS CHIN.
"YOU DO THIS, AND WE MIGHT LET YOU LIVE. DON'T DO IT, AND WE WILL DEFINITELY KILL YOU."
"SHOW ME HOW BAD YOU WANT IT, CAM," LACEY SAID.
THE COUPLE WAITED UNTIL CAM KNELT DOWN AND THEN THEY JOINED HANDS AND WALKED TOWARDS THE CHALK AND CANDLES.
CAM HELD THE KNIFE IN HIS HAND. HE HAD TWO. ONE WAS SMALL, LIKE A SCALPEL, AND THE OTHER LARGE, ALMOST A SAW BLADE. HE HELD THE SAW BLADE. HE LOOKED FROM THE BLADE TO THE BODY AND THEN LOOKED AT CLOONAN AND LACEY.

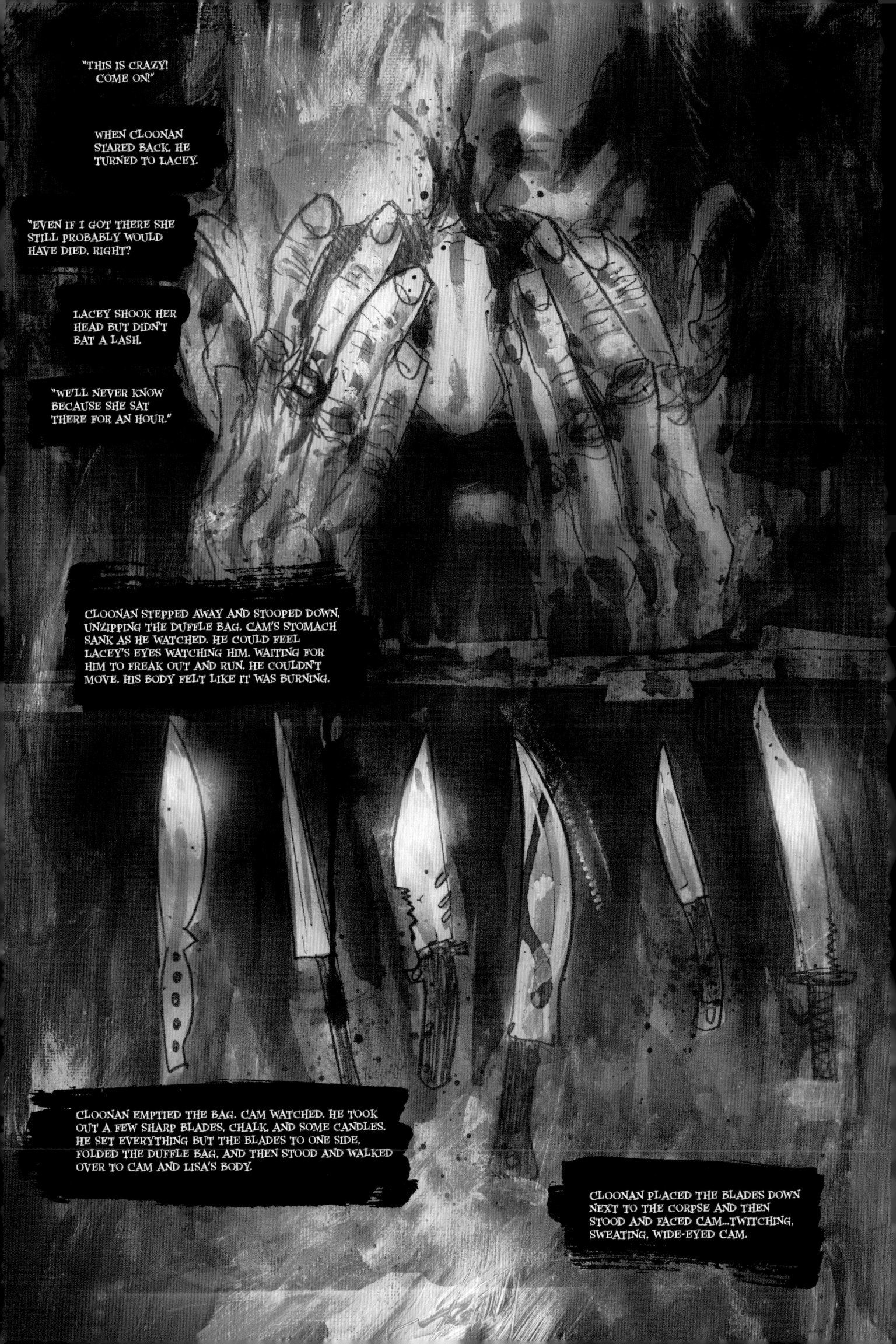

"THIS IS CRAZY! COME ON!"

WHEN CLOONAN STARED BACK, HE TURNED TO LACEY.

"EVEN IF I GOT THERE SHE STILL PROBABLY WOULD HAVE DIED, RIGHT?

LACEY SHOOK HER HEAD BUT DIDN'T BAT A LASH.

"WE'LL NEVER KNOW BECAUSE SHE SAT THERE FOR AN HOUR."

CLOONAN STEPPED AWAY AND STOOPED DOWN, UNZIPPING THE DUFFLE BAG. CAM'S STOMACH SANK AS HE WATCHED. HE COULD FEEL LACEY'S EYES WATCHING HIM, WAITING FOR HIM TO FREAK OUT AND RUN. HE COULDN'T MOVE. HIS BODY FELT LIKE IT WAS BURNING.

CLOONAN EMPTIED THE BAG. CAM WATCHED. HE TOOK OUT A FEW SHARP BLADES, CHALK, AND SOME CANDLES. HE SET EVERYTHING BUT THE BLADES TO ONE SIDE, FOLDED THE DUFFLE BAG, AND THEN STOOD AND WALKED OVER TO CAM AND LISA'S BODY.

CLOONAN PLACED THE BLADES DOWN NEXT TO THE CORPSE AND THEN STOOD AND FACED CAM...TWITCHING, SWEATING, WIDE-EYED CAM.

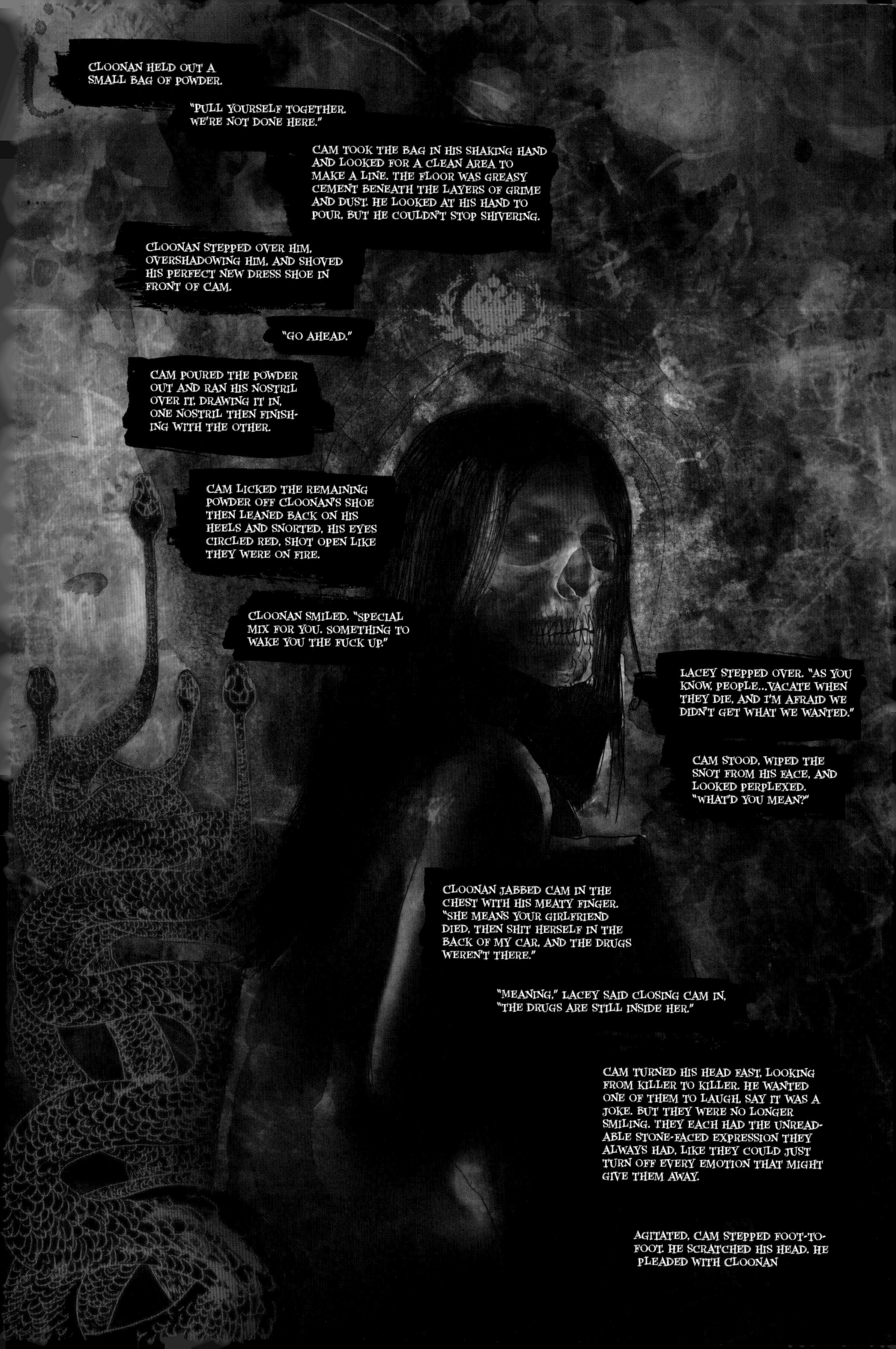
CLOONAN HELD OUT A SMALL BAG OF POWDER.
"PULL YOURSELF TOGETHER. WE'RE NOT DONE HERE."
CAM TOOK THE BAG IN HIS SHAKING HAND AND LOOKED FOR A CLEAN AREA TO MAKE A LINE. THE FLOOR WAS GREASY CEMENT BENEATH THE LAYERS OF GRIME AND DUST. HE LOOKED AT HIS HAND TO POUR, BUT HE COULDN'T STOP SHIVERING.
CLOONAN STEPPED OVER HIM, OVERSHADOWING HIM, AND SHOVED HIS PERFECT NEW DRESS SHOE IN FRONT OF CAM.
"GO AHEAD."
CAM POURED THE POWDER OUT AND RAN HIS NOSTRIL OVER IT, DRAWING IT IN, ONE NOSTRIL THEN FINISHING WITH THE OTHER.
CAM LICKED THE REMAINING POWDER OFF CLOONAN'S SHOE THEN LEANED BACK ON HIS HEELS AND SNORTED, HIS EYES CIRCLED RED, SHOT OPEN LIKE THEY WERE ON FIRE.
CLOONAN SMILED. "SPECIAL MIX FOR YOU. SOMETHING TO WAKE YOU THE FUCK UP."
LACEY STEPPED OVER. "AS YOU KNOW, PEOPLE...VACATE WHEN THEY DIE, AND I'M AFRAID WE DIDN'T GET WHAT WE WANTED."
CAM STOOD, WIPED THE SNOT FROM HIS FACE, AND LOOKED PERPLEXED. "WHAT'D YOU MEAN?"
CLOONAN JABBED CAM IN THE CHEST WITH HIS MEATY FINGER. "SHE MEANS YOUR GIRLFRIEND DIED, THEN SHIT HERSELF IN THE BACK OF MY CAR, AND THE DRUGS WEREN'T THERE."
"MEANING," LACEY SAID CLOSING CAM IN, "THE DRUGS ARE STILL INSIDE HER."
CAM TURNED HIS HEAD FAST, LOOKING FROM KILLER TO KILLER. HE WANTED ONE OF THEM TO LAUGH, SAY IT WAS A JOKE. BUT THEY WERE NO LONGER SMILING. THEY EACH HAD THE UNREADABLE STONE-FACED EXPRESSION THEY ALWAYS HAD, LIKE THEY COULD JUST TURN OFF EVERY EMOTION THAT MIGHT GIVE THEM AWAY.
AGITATED, CAM STEPPED FOOT-TO-FOOT. HE SCRATCHED HIS HEAD. HE PLEADED WITH CLOONAN

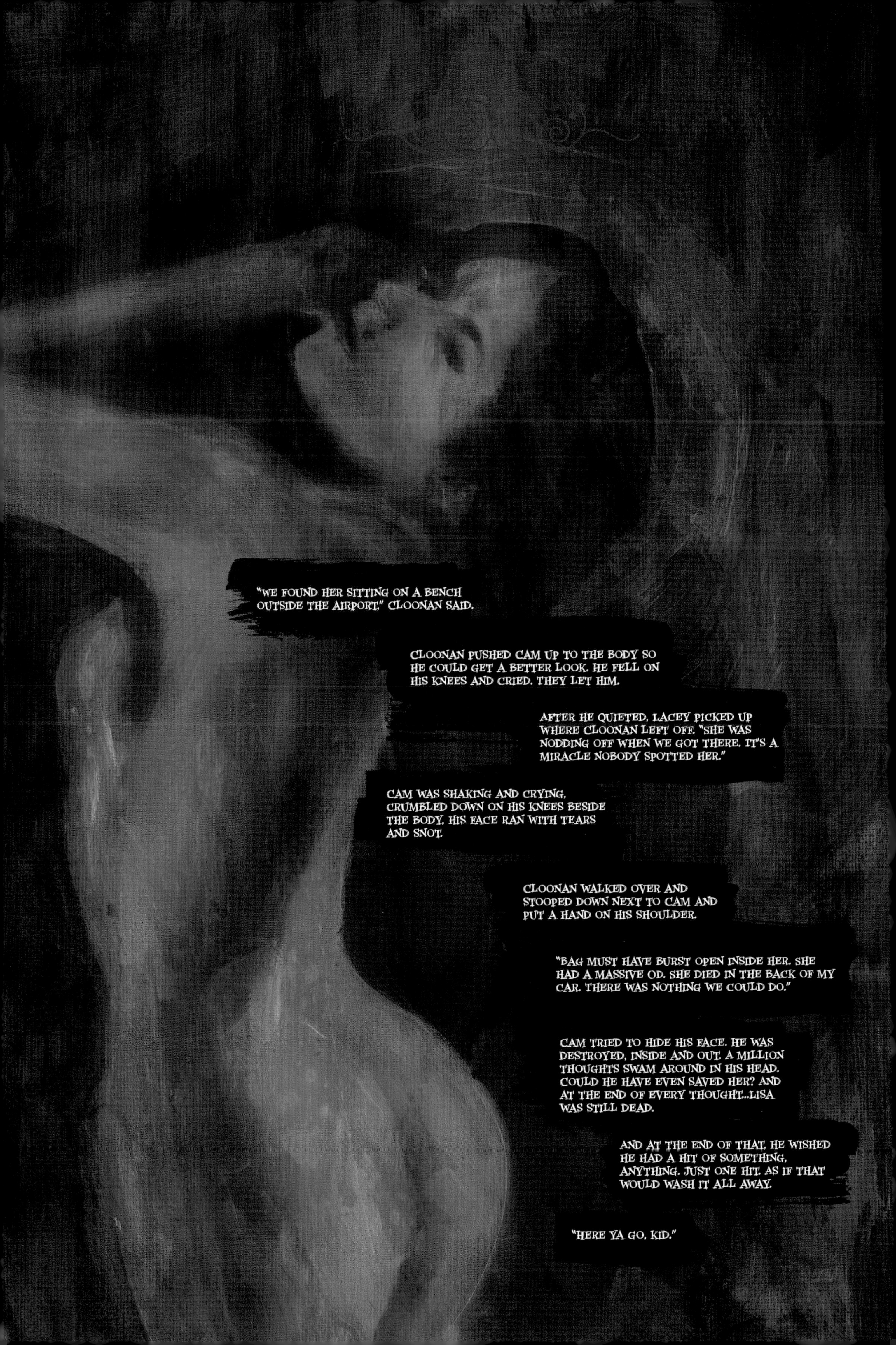
"WE FOUND HER SITTING ON A BENCH OUTSIDE THE AIRPORT," CLOONAN SAID.
CLOONAN PUSHED CAM UP TO THE BODY SO HE COULD GET A BETTER LOOK. HE FELL ON HIS KNEES AND CRIED. THEY LET HIM.
AFTER HE QUIETED, LACEY PICKED UP WHERE CLOONAN LEFT OFF. "SHE WAS NODDING OFF WHEN WE GOT THERE. IT'S A MIRACLE NOBODY SPOTTED HER."
CAM WAS SHAKING AND CRYING, CRUMBLED DOWN ON HIS KNEES BESIDE THE BODY, HIS FACE RAN WITH TEARS AND SNOT.
CLOONAN WALKED OVER AND STOOPED DOWN NEXT TO CAM AND PUT A HAND ON HIS SHOULDER.
"BAG MUST HAVE BURST OPEN INSIDE HER. SHE HAD A MASSIVE OD. SHE DIED IN THE BACK OF MY CAR. THERE WAS NOTHING WE COULD DO."
CAM TRIED TO HIDE HIS FACE. HE WAS DESTROYED, INSIDE AND OUT. A MILLION THOUGHTS SWAM AROUND IN HIS HEAD. COULD HE HAVE EVEN SAVED HER? AND AT THE END OF EVERY THOUGHT...LISA WAS STILL DEAD.
AND AT THE END OF THAT, HE WISHED HE HAD A HIT OF SOMETHING, ANYTHING. JUST ONE HIT. AS IF THAT WOULD WASH IT ALL AWAY.
"HERE YA GO, KID."

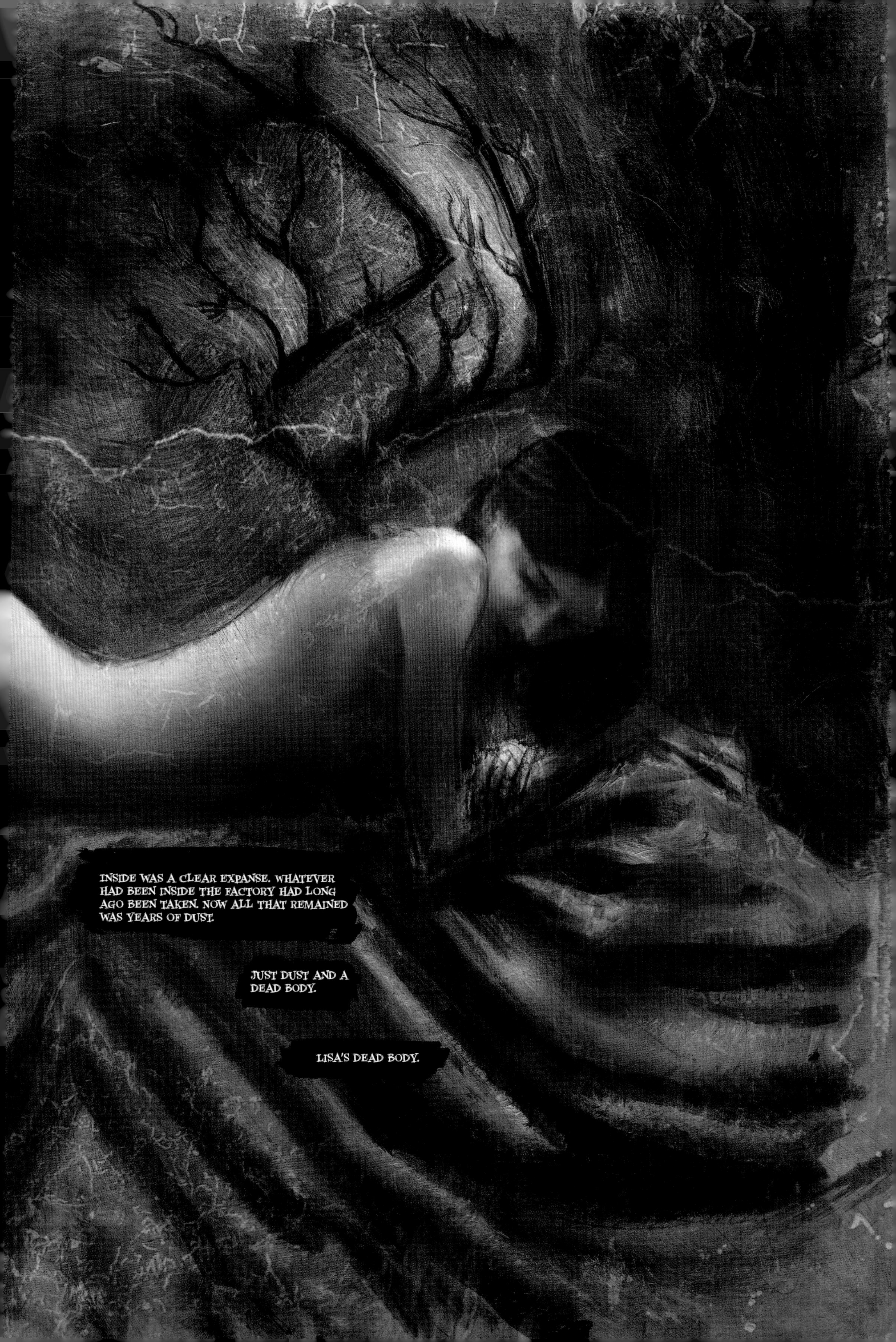
INSIDE WAS A CLEAR EXPANSE. WHATEVER HAD BEEN INSIDE THE FACTORY HAD LONG AGO BEEN TAKEN. NOW ALL THAT REMAINED WAS YEARS OF DUST.
JUST DUST AND A DEAD BODY.
LISA'S DEAD BODY.

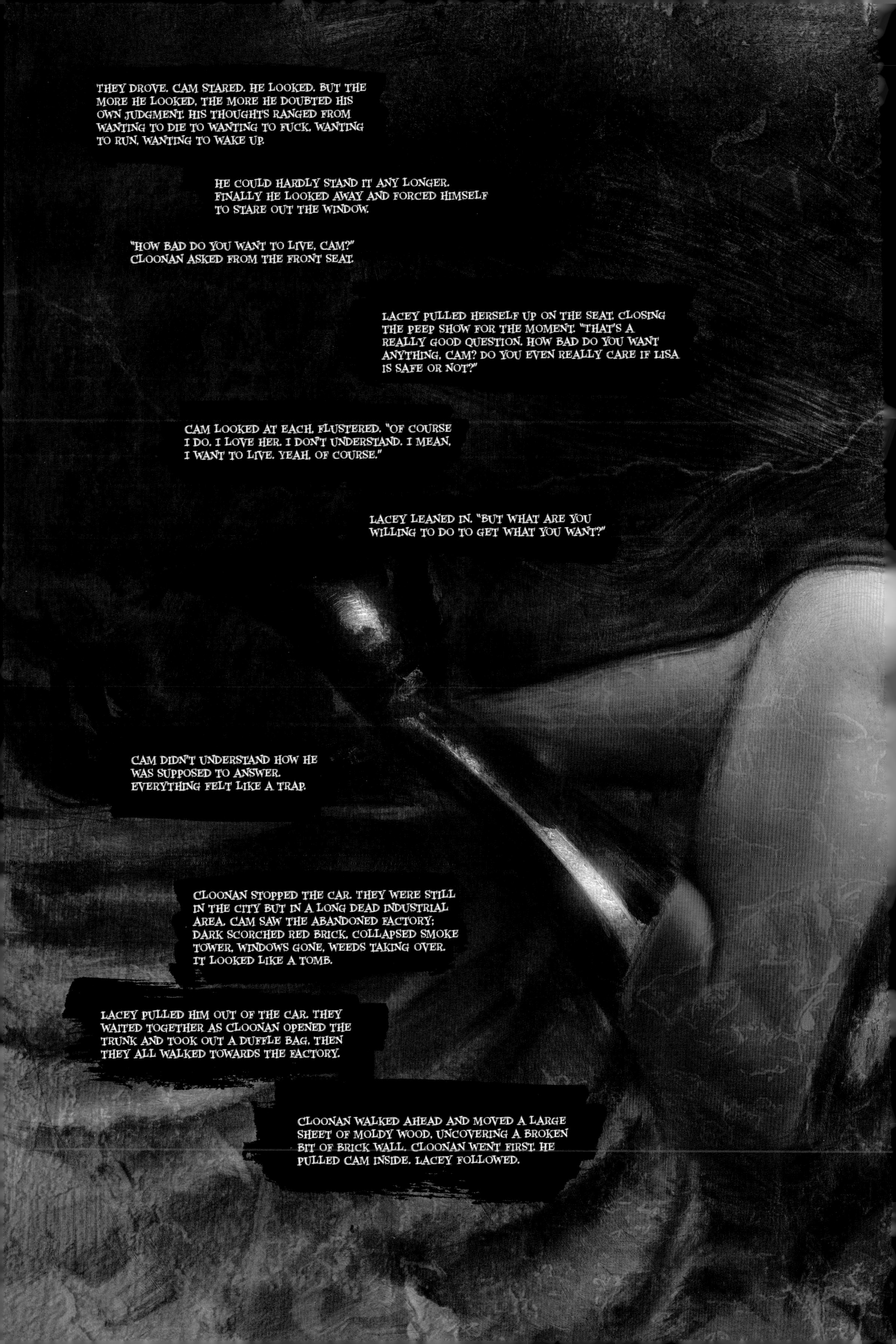
THEY DROVE. CAM STARED. HE LOOKED. BUT THE MORE HE LOOKED, THE MORE HE DOUBTED HIS OWN JUDGMENT. HIS THOUGHTS RANGED FROM WANTING TO DIE TO WANTING TO FUCK, WANTING TO RUN, WANTING TO WAKE UP.
HE COULD HARDLY STAND IT ANY LONGER. FINALLY HE LOOKED AWAY AND FORCED HIMSELF TO STARE OUT THE WINDOW.
"HOW BAD DO YOU WANT TO LIVE, CAM?" CLOONAN ASKED FROM THE FRONT SEAT.
LACEY PULLED HERSELF UP ON THE SEAT, CLOSING THE PEEP SHOW FOR THE MOMENT. "THAT'S A REALLY GOOD QUESTION. HOW BAD DO YOU WANT ANYTHING, CAM? DO YOU EVEN REALLY CARE IF LISA IS SAFE OR NOT?"
CAM LOOKED AT EACH, FLUSTERED. "OF COURSE I DO. I LOVE HER. I DON'T UNDERSTAND. I MEAN, I WANT TO LIVE. YEAH, OF COURSE."
LACEY LEANED IN. "BUT WHAT ARE YOU WILLING TO DO TO GET WHAT YOU WANT?"
CAM DIDN'T UNDERSTAND HOW HE WAS SUPPOSED TO ANSWER. EVERYTHING FELT LIKE A TRAP.
CLOONAN STOPPED THE CAR. THEY WERE STILL IN THE CITY BUT IN A LONG DEAD INDUSTRIAL AREA. CAM SAW THE ABANDONED FACTORY: DARK SCORCHED RED BRICK, COLLAPSED SMOKE TOWER, WINDOWS GONE, WEEDS TAKING OVER. IT LOOKED LIKE A TOMB.
LACEY PULLED HIM OUT OF THE CAR. THEY WAITED TOGETHER AS CLOONAN OPENED THE TRUNK AND TOOK OUT A DUFFLE BAG, THEN THEY ALL WALKED TOWARDS THE FACTORY.
CLOONAN WALKED AHEAD AND MOVED A LARGE SHEET OF MOLDY WOOD, UNCOVERING A BROKEN BIT OF BRICK WALL. CLOONAN WENT FIRST. HE PULLED CAM INSIDE. LACEY FOLLOWED.

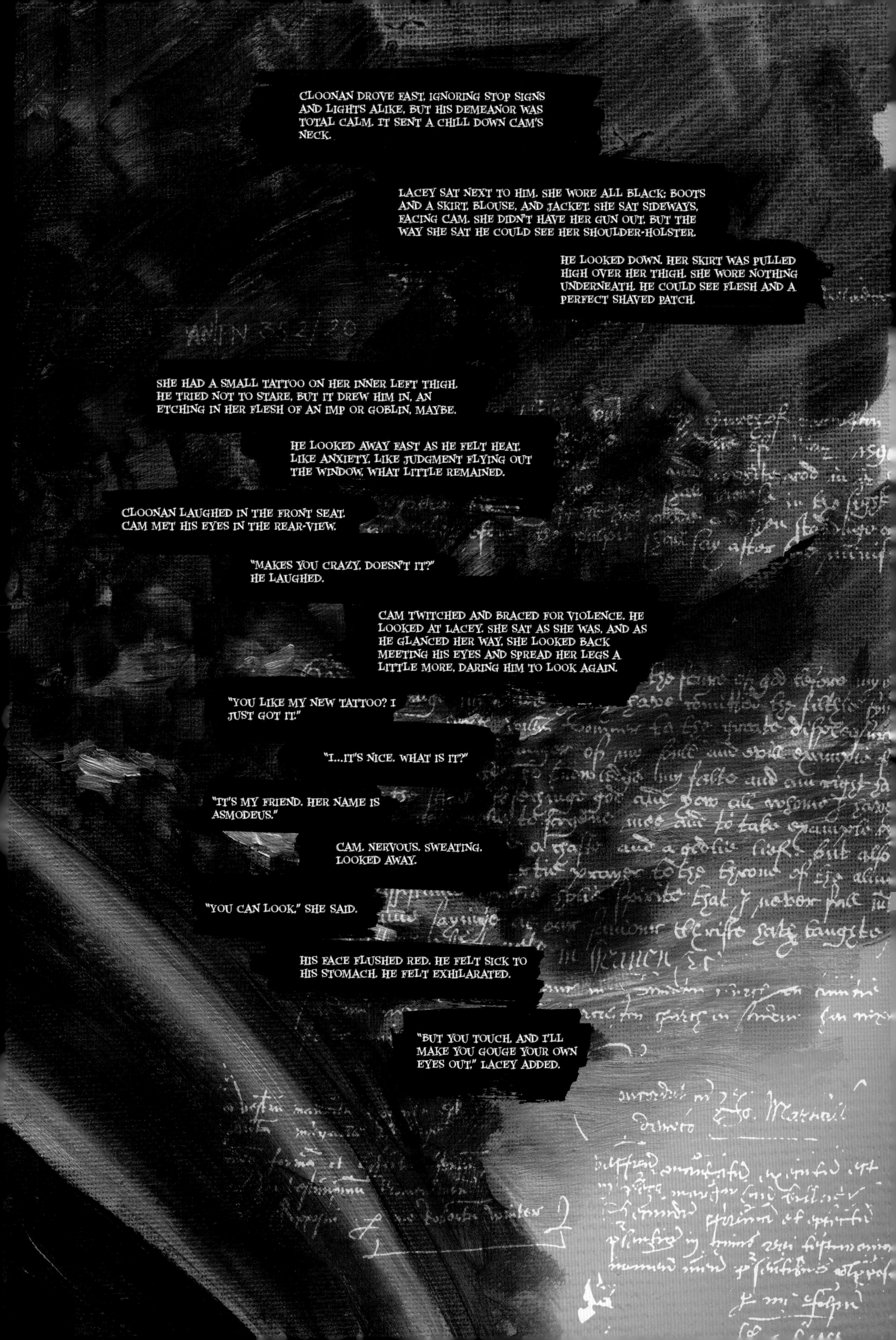
CLOONAN DROVE EAST, IGNORING STOP SIGNS AND LIGHTS ALIKE, BUT HIS DEMEANOR WAS TOTAL CALM. IT SENT A CHILL DOWN CAM'S NECK.
LACEY SAT NEXT TO HIM. SHE WORE ALL BLACK: BOOTS AND A SKIRT, BLOUSE, AND JACKET. SHE SAT SIDEWAYS, FACING CAM. SHE DIDN'T HAVE HER GUN OUT, BUT THE WAY SHE SAT HE COULD SEE HER SHOULDER-HOLSTER.
HE LOOKED DOWN. HER SKIRT WAS PULLED HIGH OVER HER THIGH. SHE WORE NOTHING UNDERNEATH. HE COULD SEE FLESH AND A PERFECT SHAVED PATCH.
SHE HAD A SMALL TATTOO ON HER INNER LEFT THIGH. HE TRIED NOT TO STARE, BUT IT DREW HIM IN, AN ETCHING IN HER FLESH OF AN IMP OR GOBLIN, MAYBE.
HE LOOKED AWAY FAST AS HE FELT HEAT, LIKE ANXIETY, LIKE JUDGMENT FLYING OUT THE WINDOW, WHAT LITTLE REMAINED.
CLOONAN LAUGHED IN THE FRONT SEAT. CAM MET HIS EYES IN THE REAR-VIEW.
"MAKES YOU CRAZY, DOESN'T IT?" HE LAUGHED.
CAM TWITCHED AND BRACED FOR VIOLENCE. HE LOOKED AT LACEY. SHE SAT AS SHE WAS, AND AS HE GLANCED HER WAY, SHE LOOKED BACK MEETING HIS EYES AND SPREAD HER LEGS A LITTLE MORE, DARING HIM TO LOOK AGAIN.
"YOU LIKE MY NEW TATTOO? I JUST GOT IT."
"I...IT'S NICE. WHAT IS IT?"
"IT'S MY FRIEND. HER NAME IS ASMODEUS."
CAM. NERVOUS. SWEATING. LOOKED AWAY.
"YOU CAN LOOK," SHE SAID.
HIS FACE FLUSHED RED. HE FELT SICK TO HIS STOMACH. HE FELT EXHILARATED.
"BUT YOU TOUCH, AND I'LL MAKE YOU GOUGE YOUR OWN EYES OUT," LACEY ADDED.

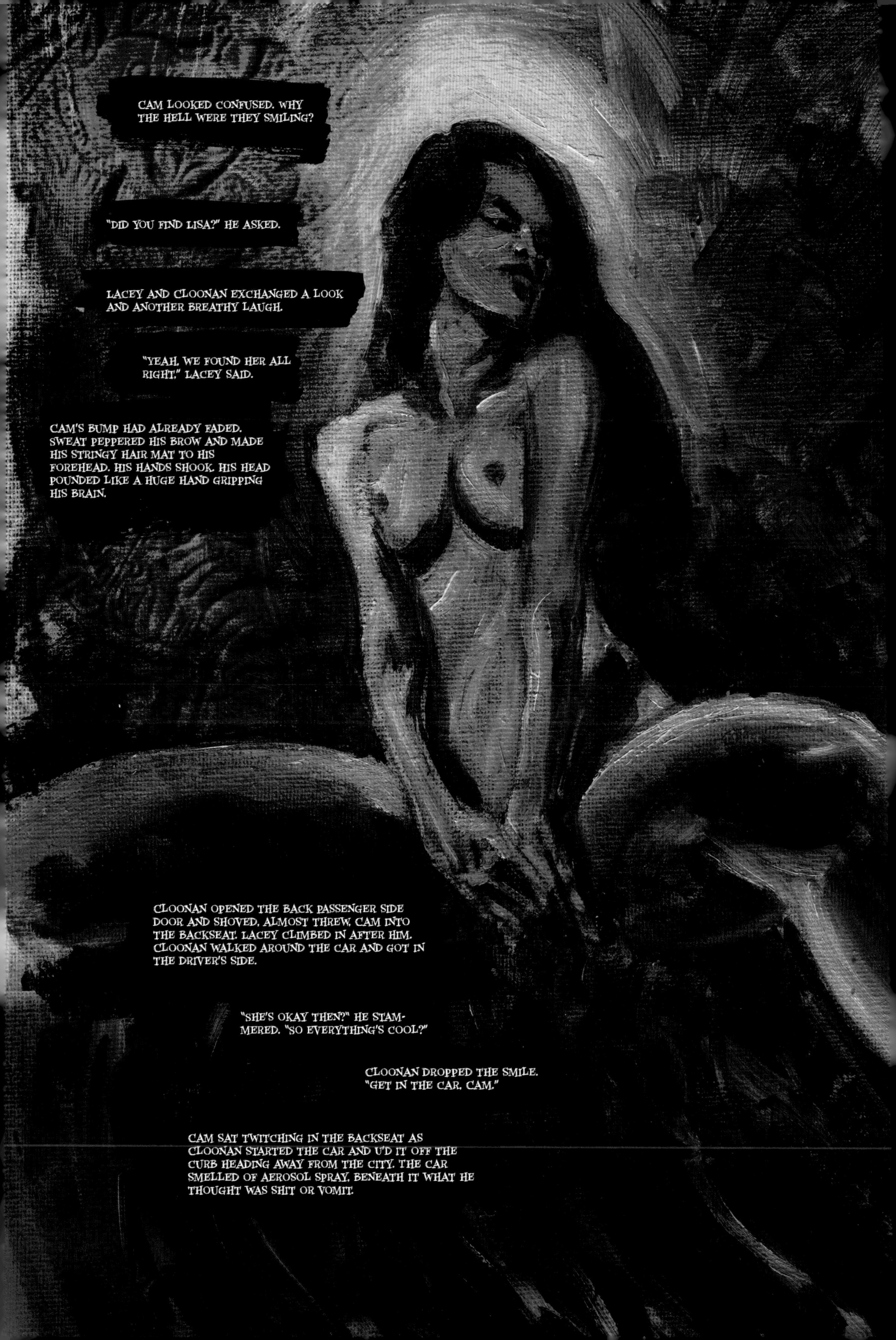

CAM LOOKED CONFUSED. WHY THE HELL WERE THEY SMILING?

"DID YOU FIND LISA?" HE ASKED.

LACEY AND CLOONAN EXCHANGED A LOOK AND ANOTHER BREATHY LAUGH.

"YEAH, WE FOUND HER ALL RIGHT," LACEY SAID.

CAM'S BUMP HAD ALREADY FADED. SWEAT PEPPERED HIS BROW AND MADE HIS STRINGY HAIR MAT TO HIS FOREHEAD. HIS HANDS SHOOK. HIS HEAD POUNDED LIKE A HUGE HAND GRIPPING HIS BRAIN.

CLOONAN OPENED THE BACK PASSENGER SIDE DOOR AND SHOVED, ALMOST THREW, CAM INTO THE BACKSEAT. LACEY CLIMBED IN AFTER HIM. CLOONAN WALKED AROUND THE CAR AND GOT IN THE DRIVER'S SIDE.

"SHE'S OKAY THEN?" HE STAMMERED. "SO EVERYTHING'S COOL?"

CLOONAN DROPPED THE SMILE. "GET IN THE CAR, CAM."

CAM SAT TWITCHING IN THE BACKSEAT AS CLOONAN STARTED THE CAR AND U'D IT OFF THE CURB HEADING AWAY FROM THE CITY. THE CAR SMELLED OF AEROSOL SPRAY, BENEATH IT WHAT HE THOUGHT WAS SHIT OR VOMIT.

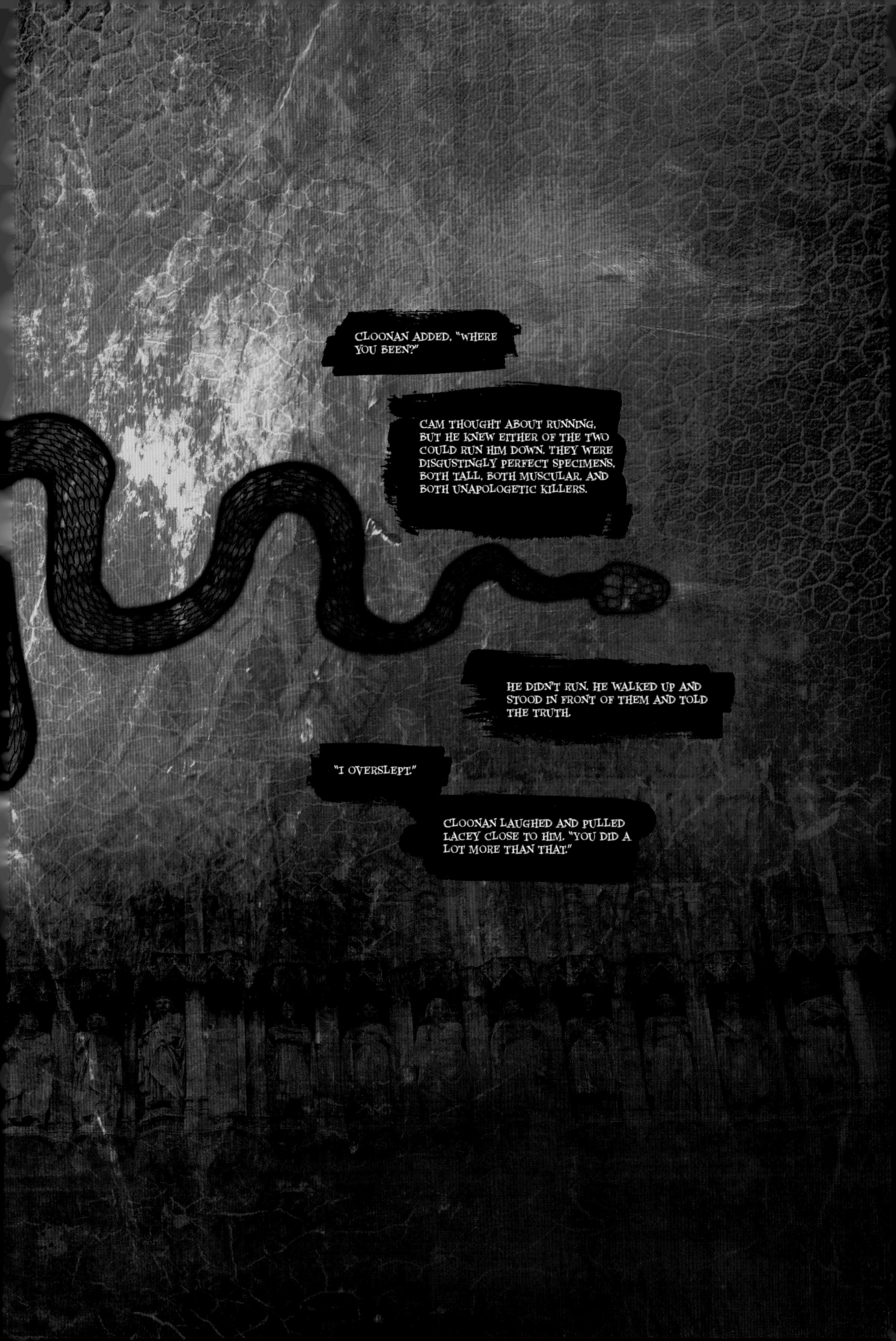

CLOONAN ADDED, "WHERE YOU BEEN?"

CAM THOUGHT ABOUT RUNNING, BUT HE KNEW EITHER OF THE TWO COULD RUN HIM DOWN. THEY WERE DISGUSTINGLY PERFECT SPECIMENS, BOTH TALL, BOTH MUSCULAR, AND BOTH UNAPOLOGETIC KILLERS.

HE DIDN'T RUN. HE WALKED UP AND STOOD IN FRONT OF THEM AND TOLD THE TRUTH.

"I OVERSLEPT."

CLOONAN LAUGHED AND PULLED LACEY CLOSE TO HIM. "YOU DID A LOT MORE THAN THAT."

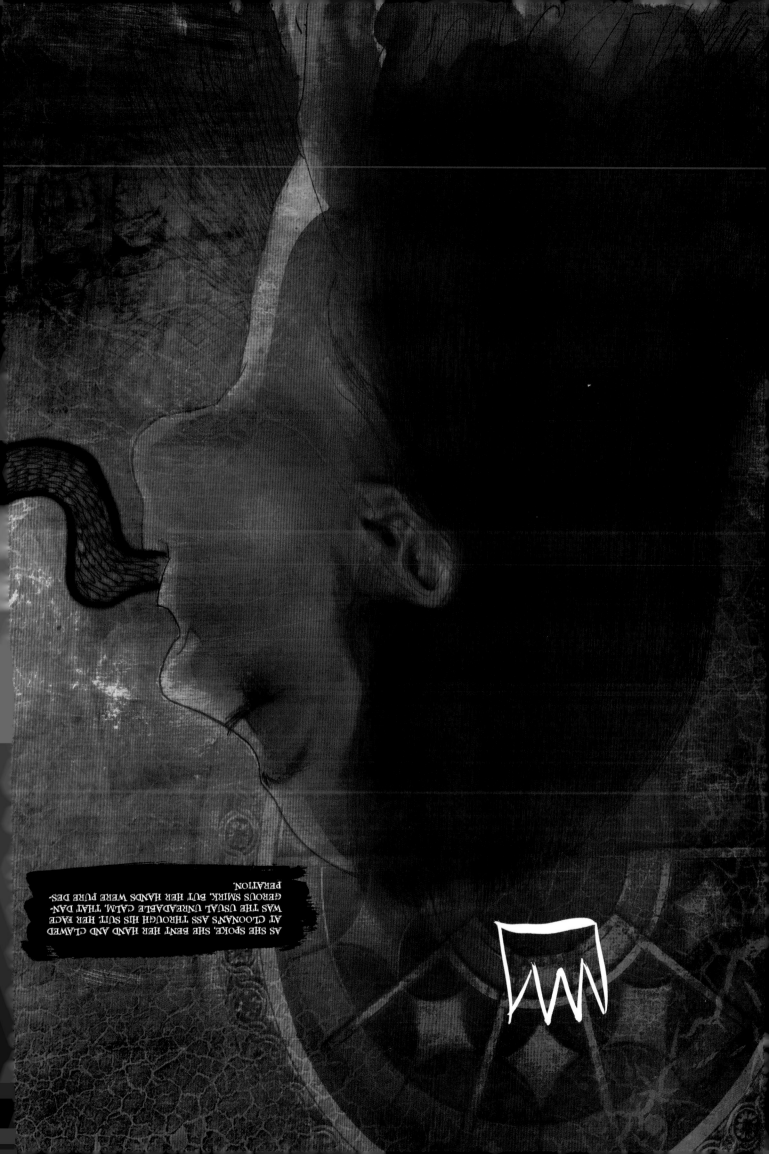

As she spoke, she bent her hand and clawed at Gloonan's ass through his suit. Her face was the usual unreadable calm, that dangerous smirk, but her hands were pure desperation.

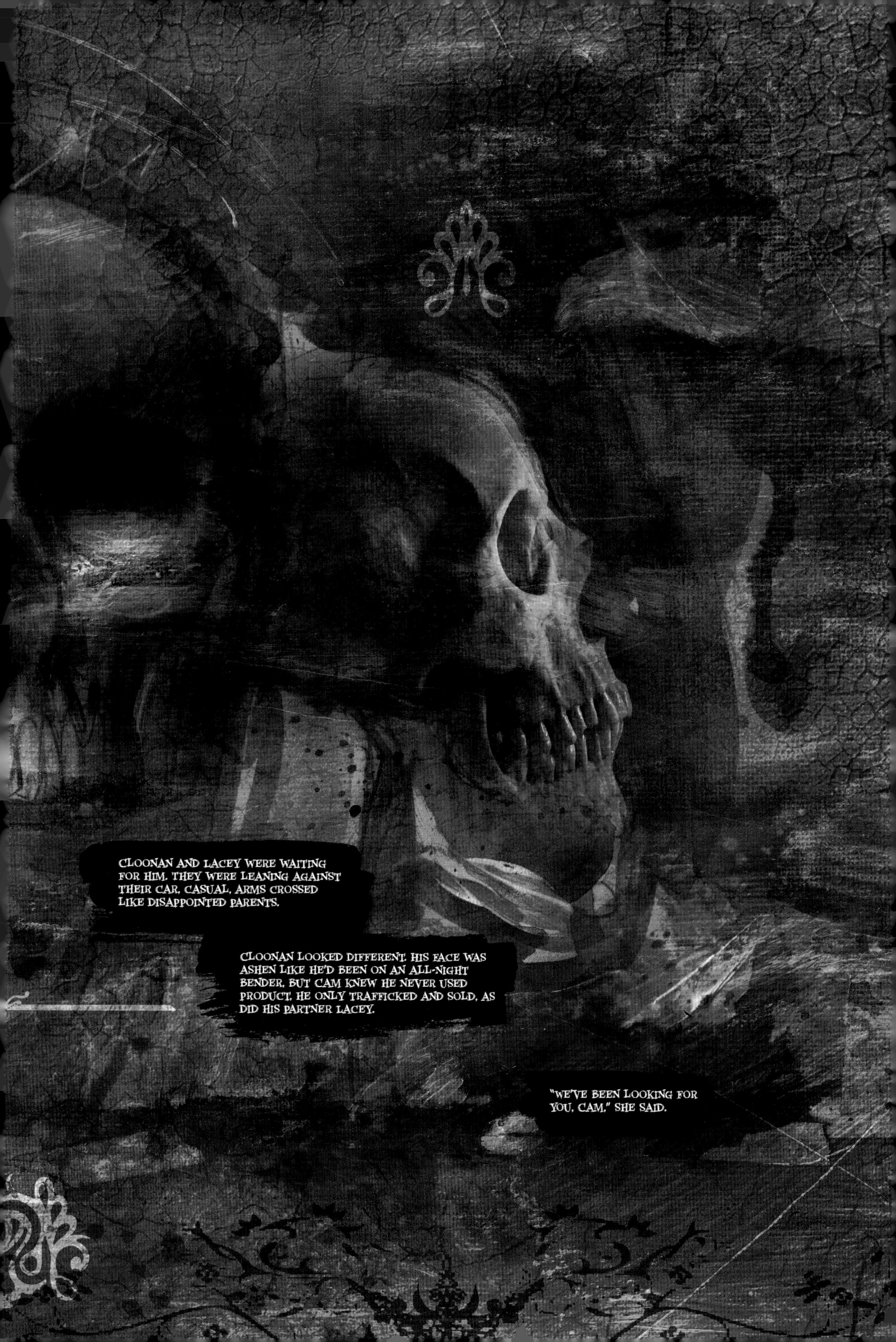
CLOONAN AND LACEY WERE WAITING FOR HIM. THEY WERE LEANING AGAINST THEIR CAR, CASUAL, ARMS CROSSED LIKE DISAPPOINTED PARENTS.
CLOONAN LOOKED DIFFERENT. HIS FACE WAS ASHEN LIKE HE'D BEEN ON AN ALL-NIGHT BENDER, BUT CAM KNEW HE NEVER USED PRODUCT. HE ONLY TRAFFICKED AND SOLD, AS DID HIS PARTNER LACEY.
"WE'VE BEEN LOOKING FOR YOU, CAM," SHE SAID.

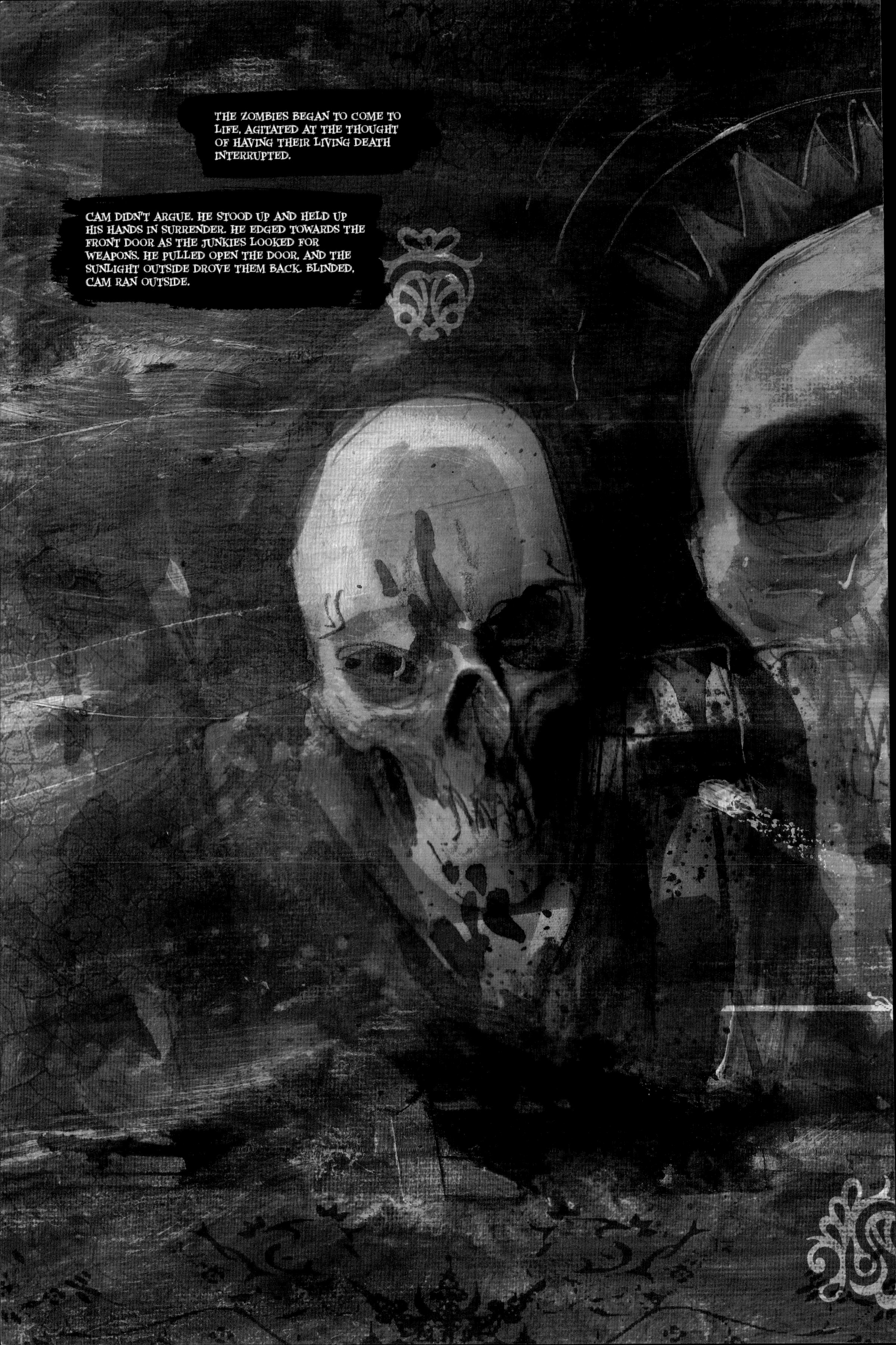
THE ZOMBIES BEGAN TO COME TO LIFE, AGITATED AT THE THOUGHT OF HAVING THEIR LIVING DEATH INTERRUPTED.
CAM DIDN'T ARGUE. HE STOOD UP AND HELD UP HIS HANDS IN SURRENDER. HE EDGED TOWARDS THE FRONT DOOR AS THE JUNKIES LOOKED FOR WEAPONS. HE PULLED OPEN THE DOOR, AND THE SUNLIGHT OUTSIDE DROVE THEM BACK. BLINDED, CAM RAN OUTSIDE.

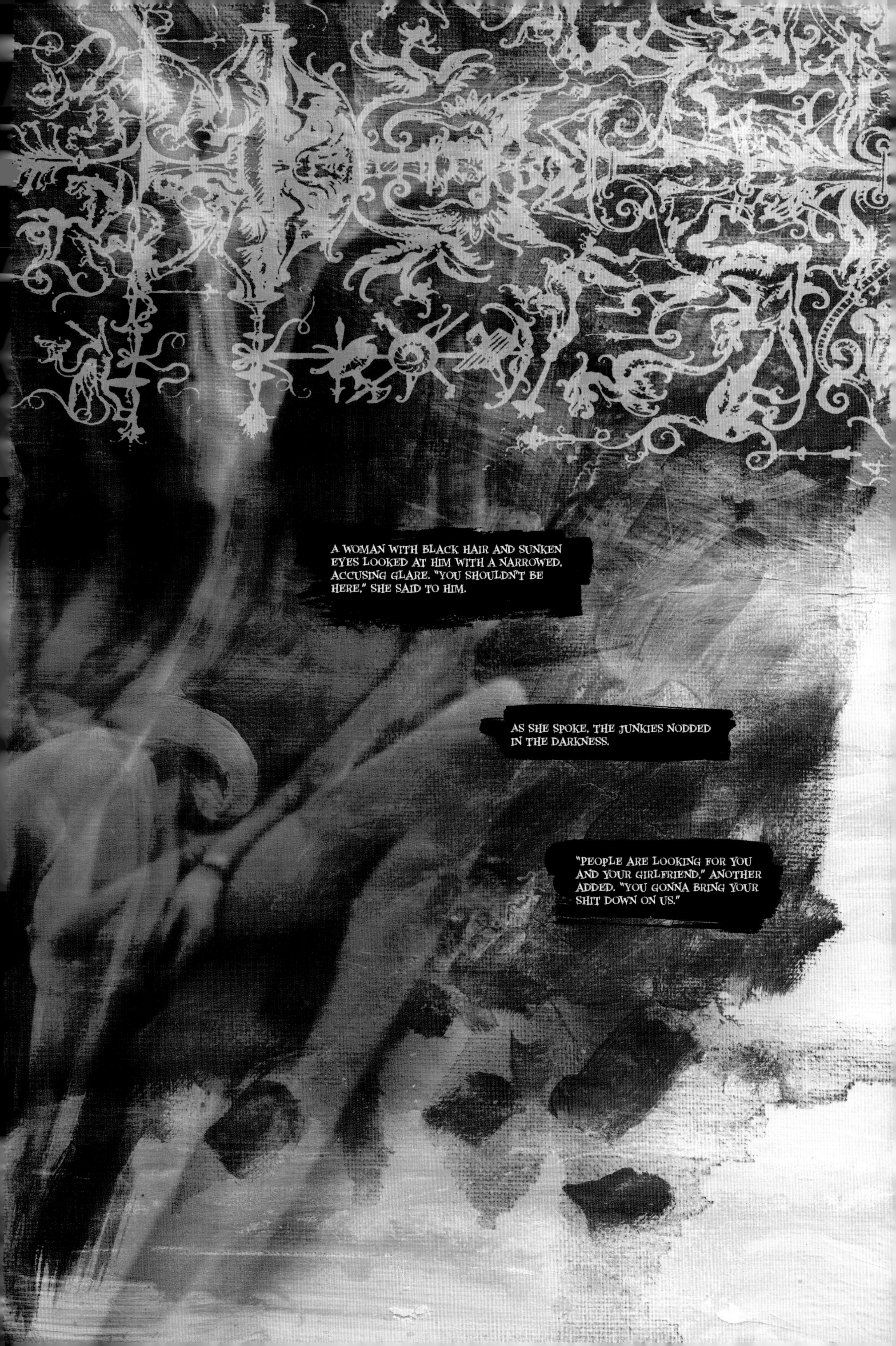
A WOMAN WITH BLACK HAIR AND SUNKEN EYES LOOKED AT HIM WITH A NARROWED, ACCUSING GLARE. "YOU SHOULDN'T BE HERE," SHE SAID TO HIM.
AS SHE SPOKE, THE JUNKIES NODDED IN THE DARKNESS.
"PEOPLE ARE LOOKING FOR YOU AND YOUR GIRLFRIEND," ANOTHER ADDED. "YOU GONNA BRING YOUR SHIT DOWN ON US."

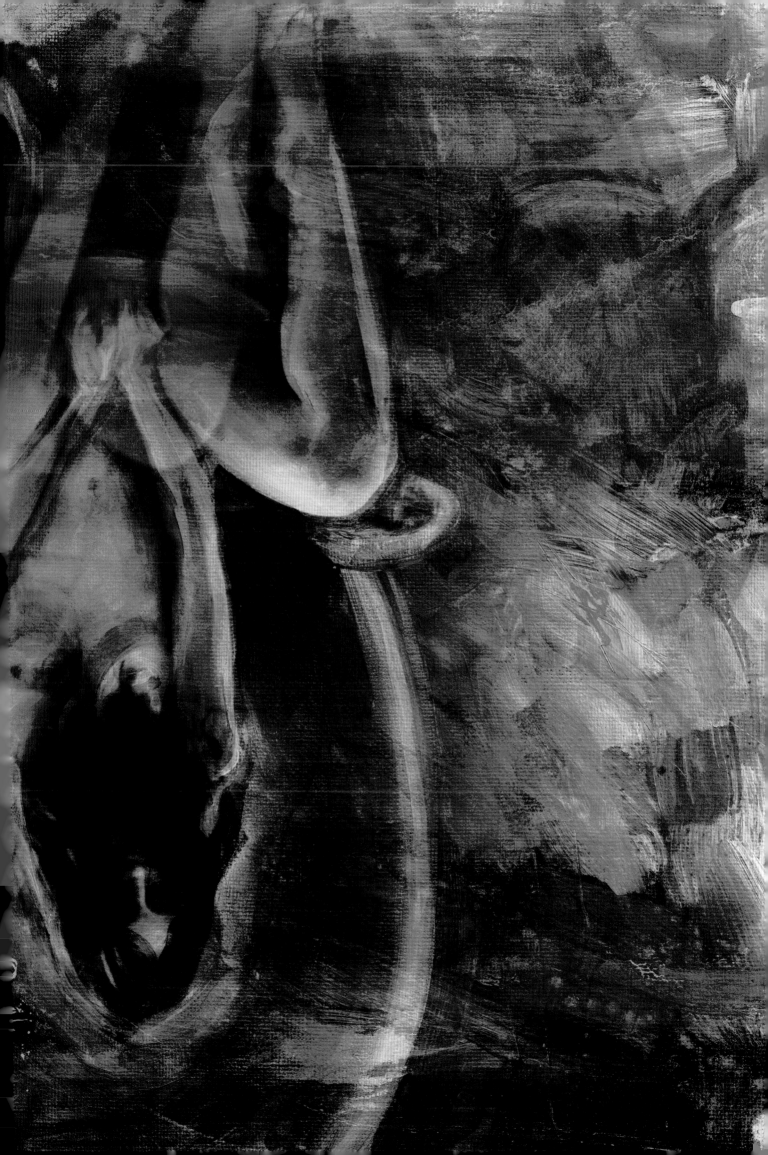

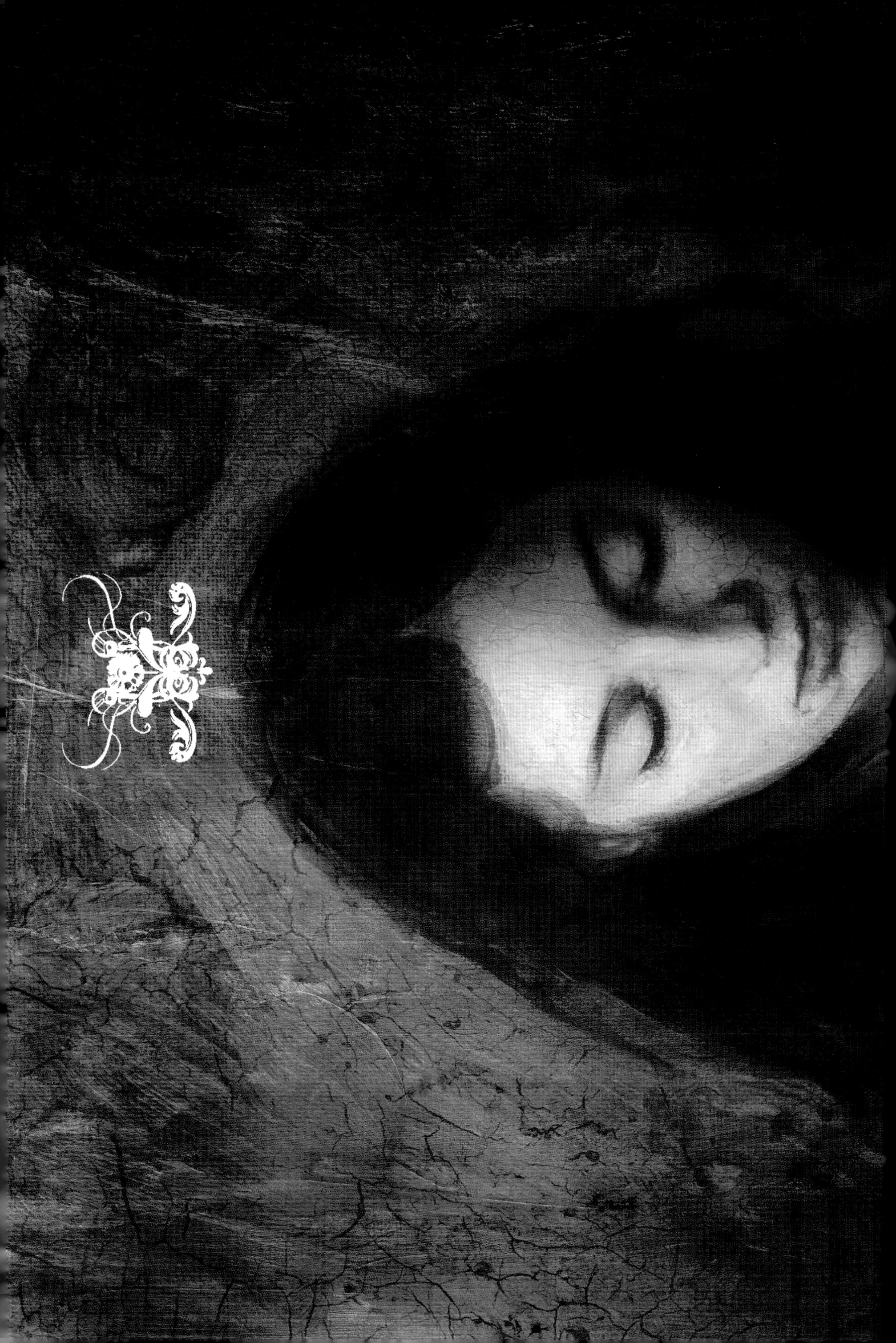

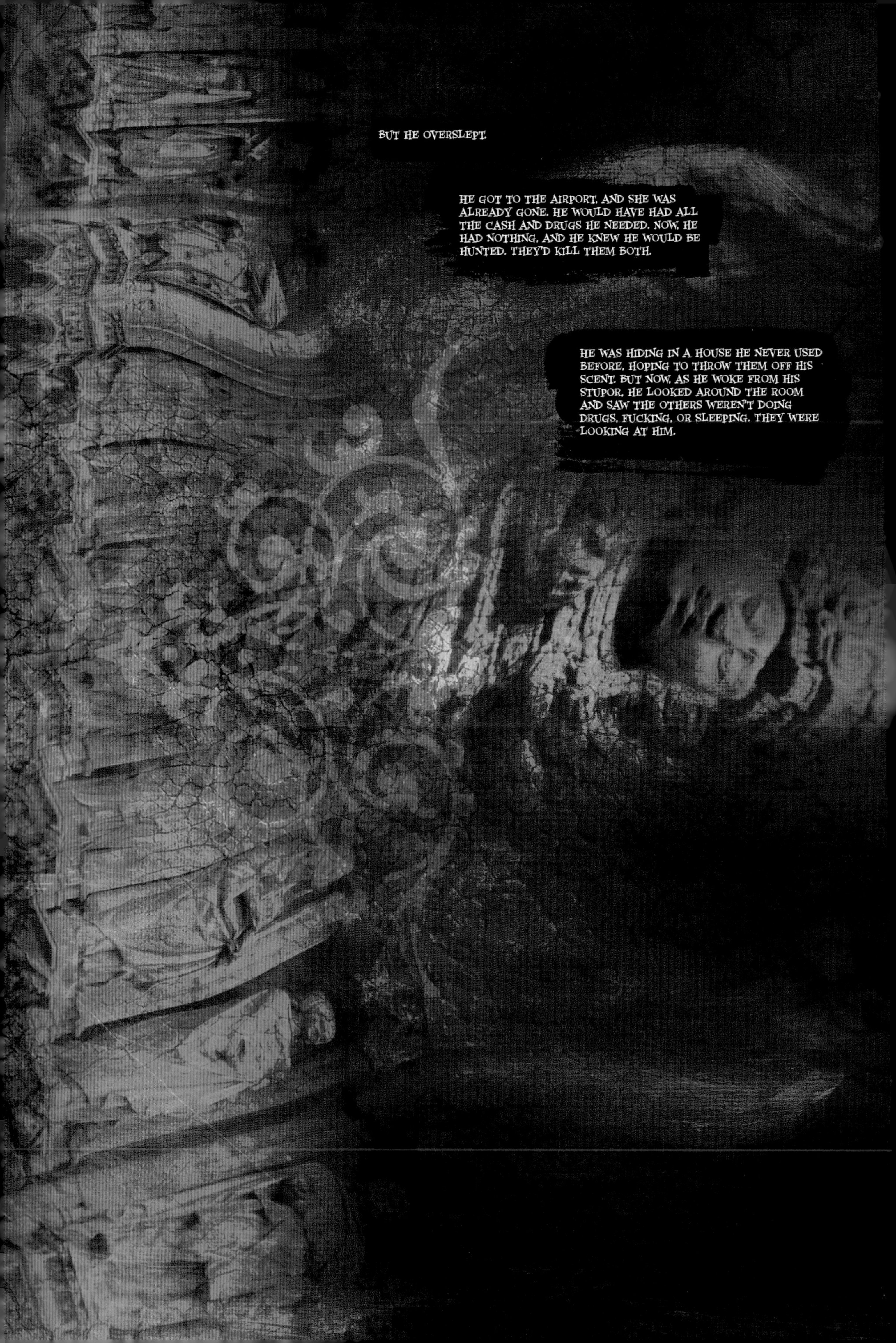
BUT HE OVERSLEPT.
HE GOT TO THE AIRPORT, AND SHE WAS ALREADY GONE. HE WOULD HAVE HAD ALL THE CASH AND DRUGS HE NEEDED. NOW, HE HAD NOTHING, AND HE KNEW HE WOULD BE HUNTED. THEY'D KILL THEM BOTH.
HE WAS HIDING IN A HOUSE HE NEVER USED BEFORE, HOPING TO THROW THEM OFF HIS SCENT. BUT NOW, AS HE WOKE FROM HIS STUPOR, HE LOOKED AROUND THE ROOM AND SAW THE OTHERS WEREN'T DOING DRUGS, FUCKING, OR SLEEPING. THEY WERE LOOKING AT HIM.

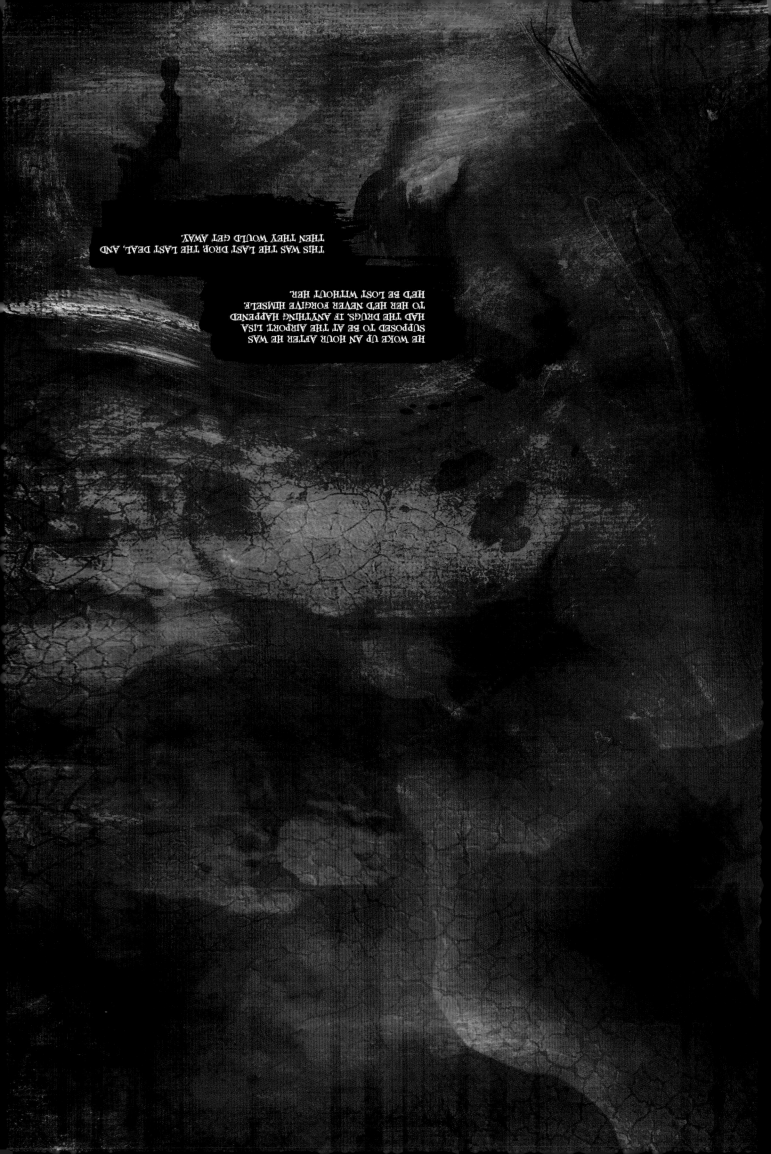

THIS WAS THE LAST DROP, THE LAST DEAL, AND
THEN THEY WOULD GET AWAY.

HE WOKE UP AN HOUR AFTER HE WAS
SUPPOSED TO BE AT THE AIRPORT. LISA
HAD THE DRUGS. IF ANYTHING HAPPENED
TO HER HE'D NEVER FORGIVE HIMSELF.
HE'D BE LOST WITHOUT HER.

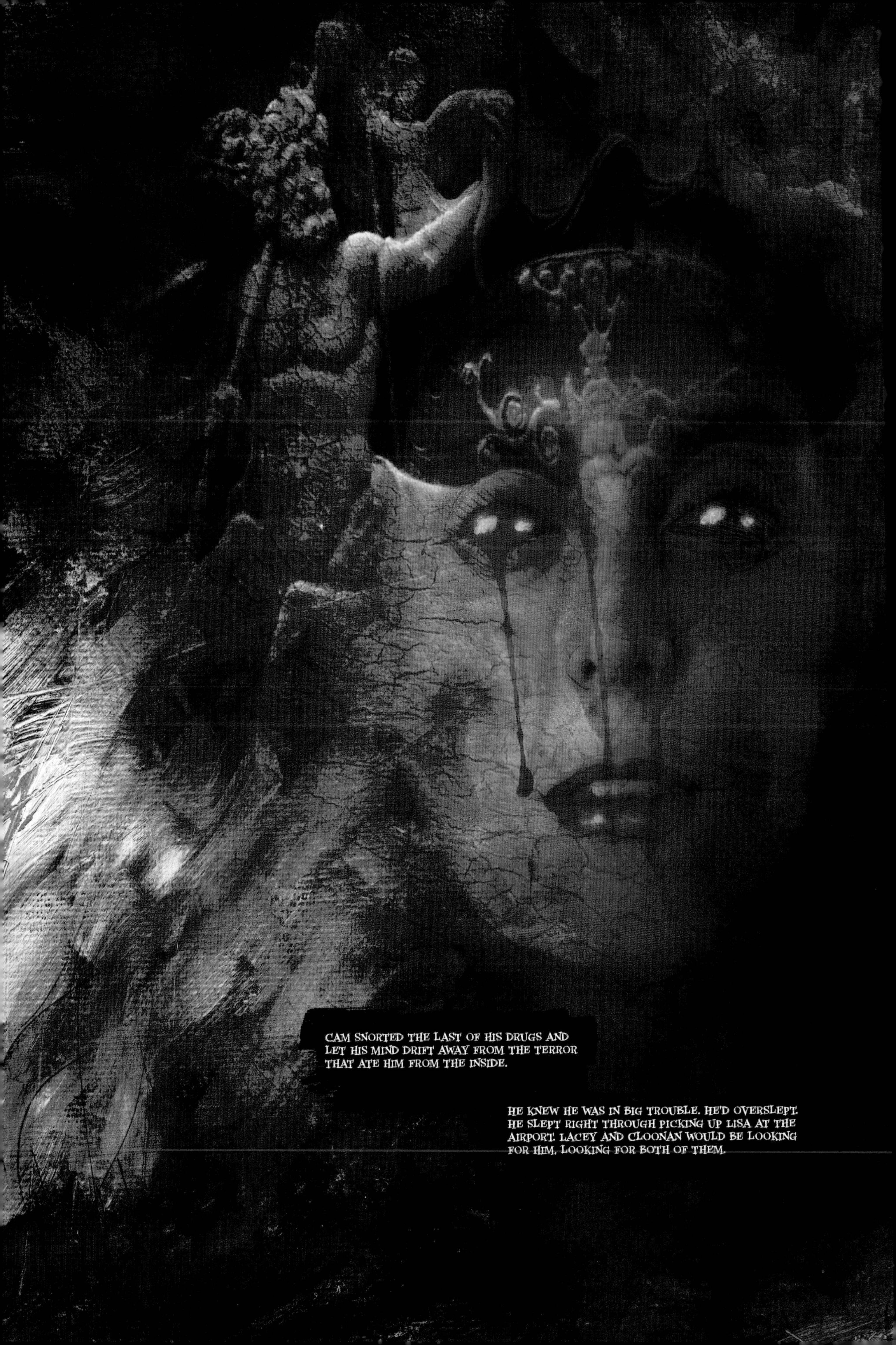
CAM SNORTED THE LAST OF HIS DRUGS AND LET HIS MIND DRIFT AWAY FROM THE TERROR THAT ATE HIM FROM THE INSIDE.
HE KNEW HE WAS IN BIG TROUBLE. HE'D OVERSLEPT. HE SLEPT RIGHT THROUGH PICKING UP LISA AT THE AIRPORT. LACEY AND CLOONAN WOULD BE LOOKING FOR HIM. LOOKING FOR BOTH OF THEM.

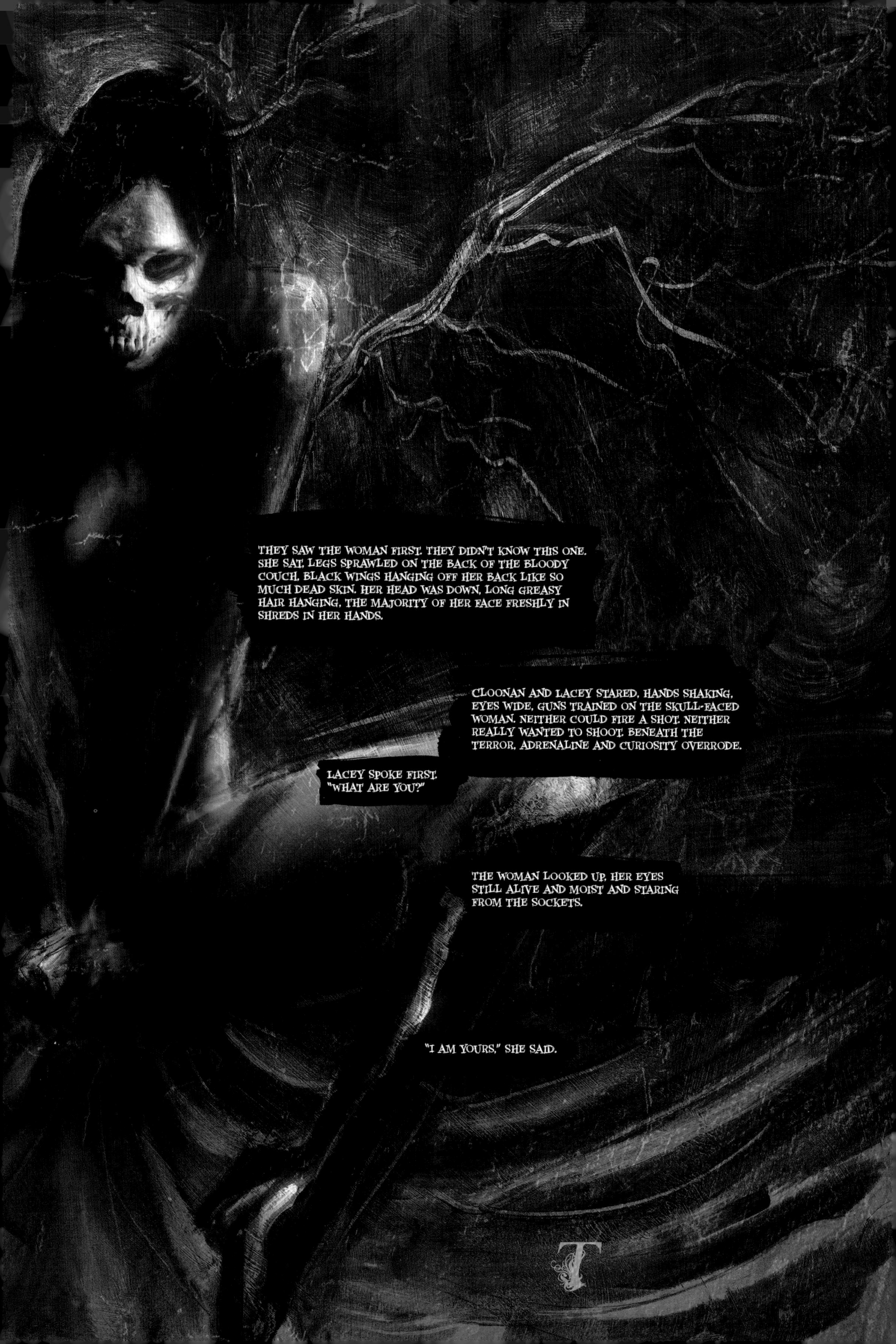
THEY SAW THE WOMAN FIRST. THEY DIDN'T KNOW THIS ONE. SHE SAT, LEGS SPRAWLED ON THE BACK OF THE BLOODY COUCH, BLACK WINGS HANGING OFF HER BACK LIKE SO MUCH DEAD SKIN. HER HEAD WAS DOWN, LONG GREASY HAIR HANGING, THE MAJORITY OF HER FACE FRESHLY IN SHREDS IN HER HANDS.
CLOONAN AND LACEY STARED, HANDS SHAKING, EYES WIDE, GUNS TRAINED ON THE SKULL-FACED WOMAN. NEITHER COULD FIRE A SHOT. NEITHER REALLY WANTED TO SHOOT. BENEATH THE TERROR, ADRENALINE AND CURIOSITY OVERRODE.
LACEY SPOKE FIRST. "WHAT ARE YOU?"
THE WOMAN LOOKED UP, HER EYES STILL ALIVE AND MOIST AND STARING FROM THE SOCKETS.
"I AM YOURS," SHE SAID.

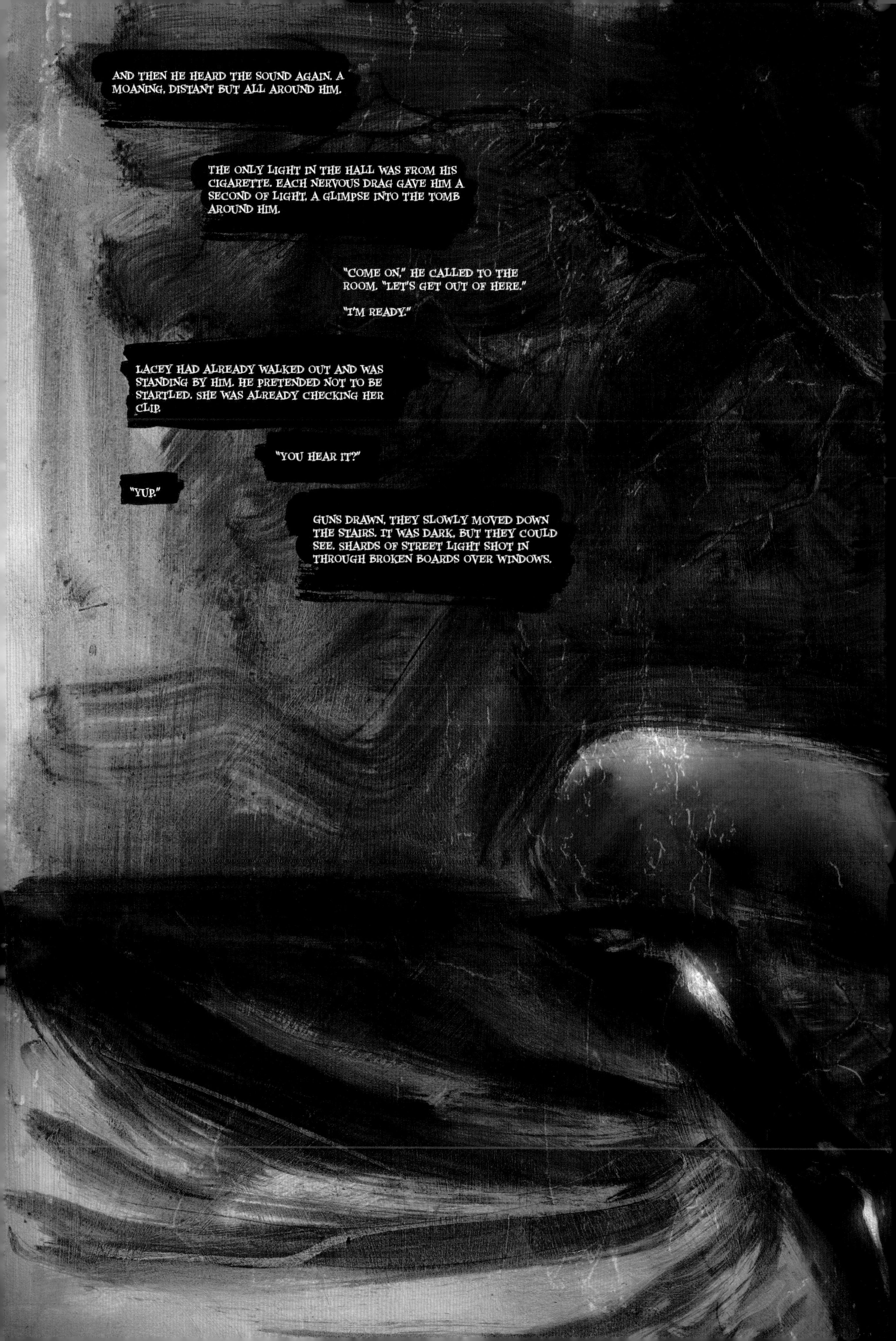
AND THEN HE HEARD THE SOUND AGAIN. A MOANING, DISTANT BUT ALL AROUND HIM.
THE ONLY LIGHT IN THE HALL WAS FROM HIS CIGARETTE. EACH NERVOUS DRAG GAVE HIM A SECOND OF LIGHT, A GLIMPSE INTO THE TOMB AROUND HIM.
"COME ON," HE CALLED TO THE ROOM. "LET'S GET OUT OF HERE."
"I'M READY."
LACEY HAD ALREADY WALKED OUT AND WAS STANDING BY HIM. HE PRETENDED NOT TO BE STARTLED. SHE WAS ALREADY CHECKING HER CLIP.
"YOU HEAR IT?"
"YUP."
GUNS DRAWN, THEY SLOWLY MOVED DOWN THE STAIRS. IT WAS DARK, BUT THEY COULD SEE. SHARDS OF STREET LIGHT SHOT IN THROUGH BROKEN BOARDS OVER WINDOWS.

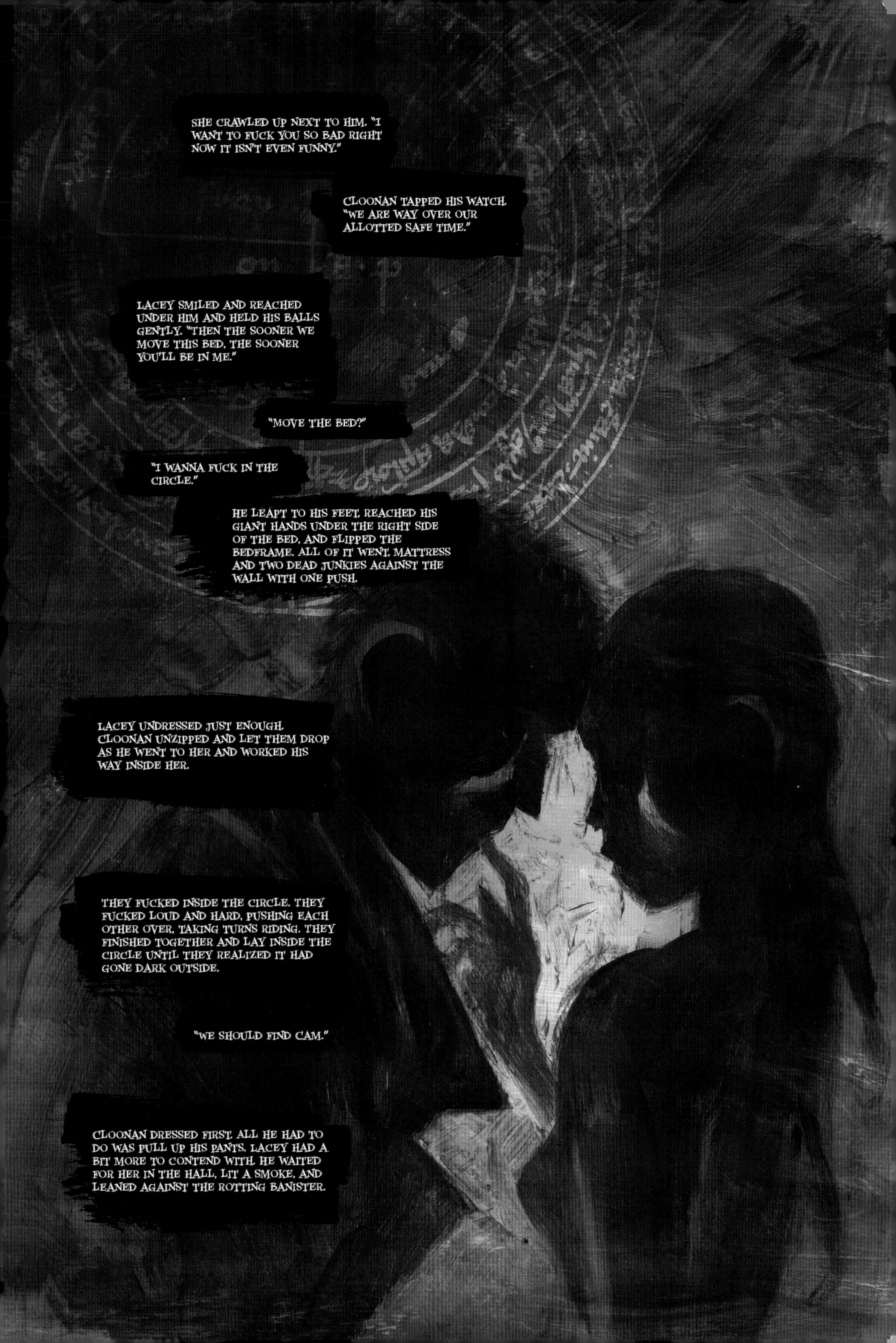
SHE CRAWLED UP NEXT TO HIM. "I WANT TO FUCK YOU SO BAD RIGHT NOW IT ISN'T EVEN FUNNY."
CLOONAN TAPPED HIS WATCH. "WE ARE WAY OVER OUR ALLOTTED SAFE TIME."
LACEY SMILED AND REACHED UNDER HIM AND HELD HIS BALLS GENTLY. "THEN THE SOONER WE MOVE THIS BED, THE SOONER YOU'LL BE IN ME."
"MOVE THE BED?"
"I WANNA FUCK IN THE CIRCLE."
HE LEAPT TO HIS FEET, REACHED HIS GIANT HANDS UNDER THE RIGHT SIDE OF THE BED, AND FLIPPED THE BEDFRAME. ALL OF IT WENT, MATTRESS AND TWO DEAD JUNKIES AGAINST THE WALL WITH ONE PUSH.
LACEY UNDRESSED JUST ENOUGH. CLOONAN UNZIPPED AND LET THEM DROP AS HE WENT TO HER AND WORKED HIS WAY INSIDE HER.
THEY FUCKED INSIDE THE CIRCLE. THEY FUCKED LOUD AND HARD, PUSHING EACH OTHER OVER, TAKING TURNS RIDING. THEY FINISHED TOGETHER AND LAY INSIDE THE CIRCLE UNTIL THEY REALIZED IT HAD GONE DARK OUTSIDE.
"WE SHOULD FIND CAM."
CLOONAN DRESSED FIRST. ALL HE HAD TO DO WAS PULL UP HIS PANTS. LACEY HAD A BIT MORE TO CONTEND WITH. HE WAITED FOR HER IN THE HALL, LIT A SMOKE, AND LEANED AGAINST THE ROTTING BANISTER.

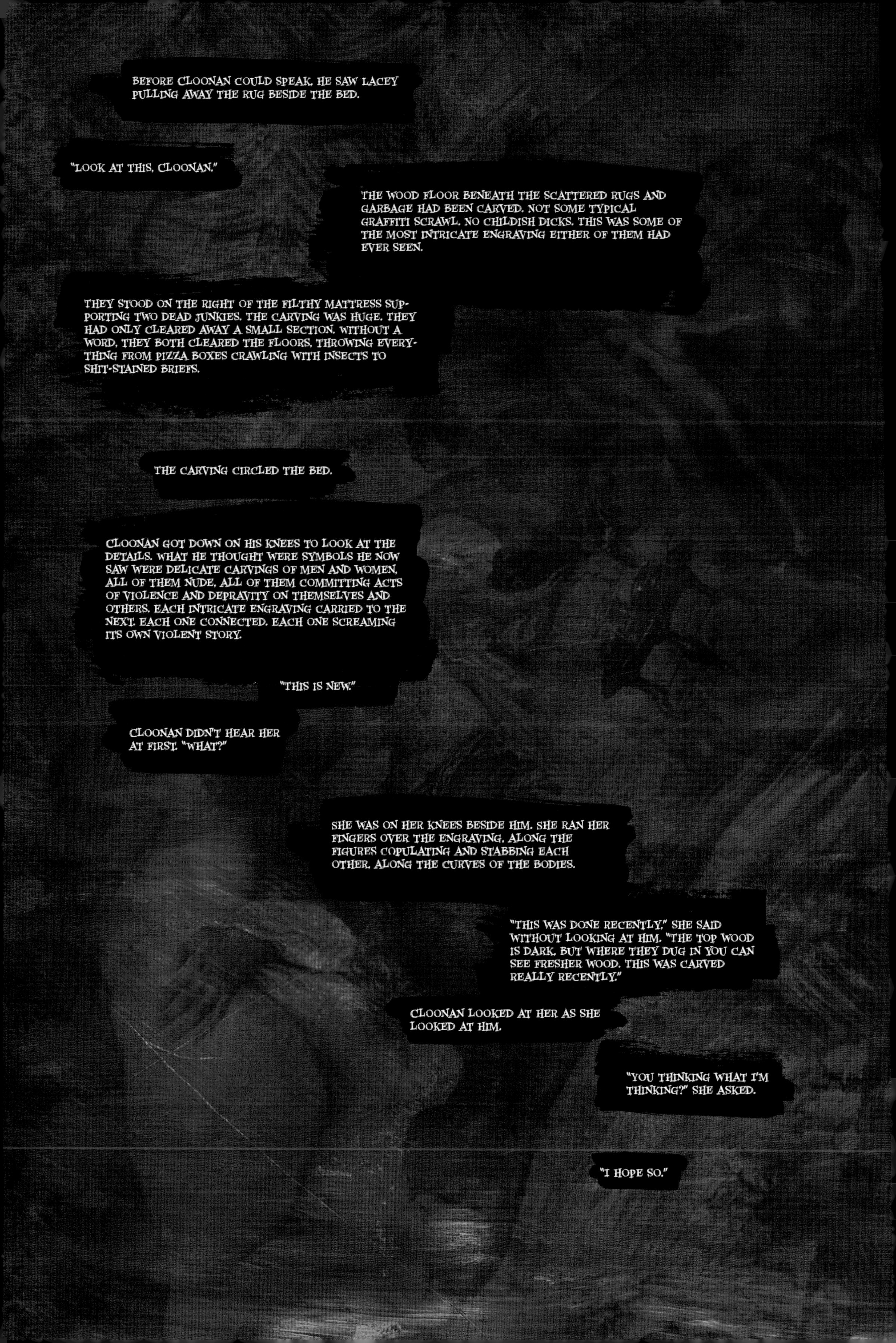
BEFORE CLOONAN COULD SPEAK, HE SAW LACEY PULLING AWAY THE RUG BESIDE THE BED.
"LOOK AT THIS, CLOONAN."
THE WOOD FLOOR BENEATH THE SCATTERED RUGS AND GARBAGE HAD BEEN CARVED. NOT SOME TYPICAL GRAFFITI SCRAWL. NO CHILDISH DICKS. THIS WAS SOME OF THE MOST INTRICATE ENGRAVING EITHER OF THEM HAD EVER SEEN.
THEY STOOD ON THE RIGHT OF THE FILTHY MATTRESS SUPPORTING TWO DEAD JUNKIES. THE CARVING WAS HUGE. THEY HAD ONLY CLEARED AWAY A SMALL SECTION. WITHOUT A WORD, THEY BOTH CLEARED THE FLOORS, THROWING EVERYTHING FROM PIZZA BOXES CRAWLING WITH INSECTS TO SHIT-STAINED BRIEFS.
THE CARVING CIRCLED THE BED.
CLOONAN GOT DOWN ON HIS KNEES TO LOOK AT THE DETAILS. WHAT HE THOUGHT WERE SYMBOLS HE NOW SAW WERE DELICATE CARVINGS OF MEN AND WOMEN, ALL OF THEM NUDE, ALL OF THEM COMMITTING ACTS OF VIOLENCE AND DEPRAVITY ON THEMSELVES AND OTHERS. EACH INTRICATE ENGRAVING CARRIED TO THE NEXT. EACH ONE CONNECTED. EACH ONE SCREAMING ITS OWN VIOLENT STORY.
"THIS IS NEW."
CLOONAN DIDN'T HEAR HER AT FIRST. "WHAT?"
SHE WAS ON HER KNEES BESIDE HIM. SHE RAN HER FINGERS OVER THE ENGRAVING, ALONG THE FIGURES COPULATING AND STABBING EACH OTHER, ALONG THE CURVES OF THE BODIES.
"THIS WAS DONE RECENTLY," SHE SAID WITHOUT LOOKING AT HIM. "THE TOP WOOD IS DARK, BUT WHERE THEY DUG IN YOU CAN SEE FRESHER WOOD. THIS WAS CARVED REALLY RECENTLY."
CLOONAN LOOKED AT HER AS SHE LOOKED AT HIM.
"YOU THINKING WHAT I'M THINKING?" SHE ASKED.
"I HOPE SO."

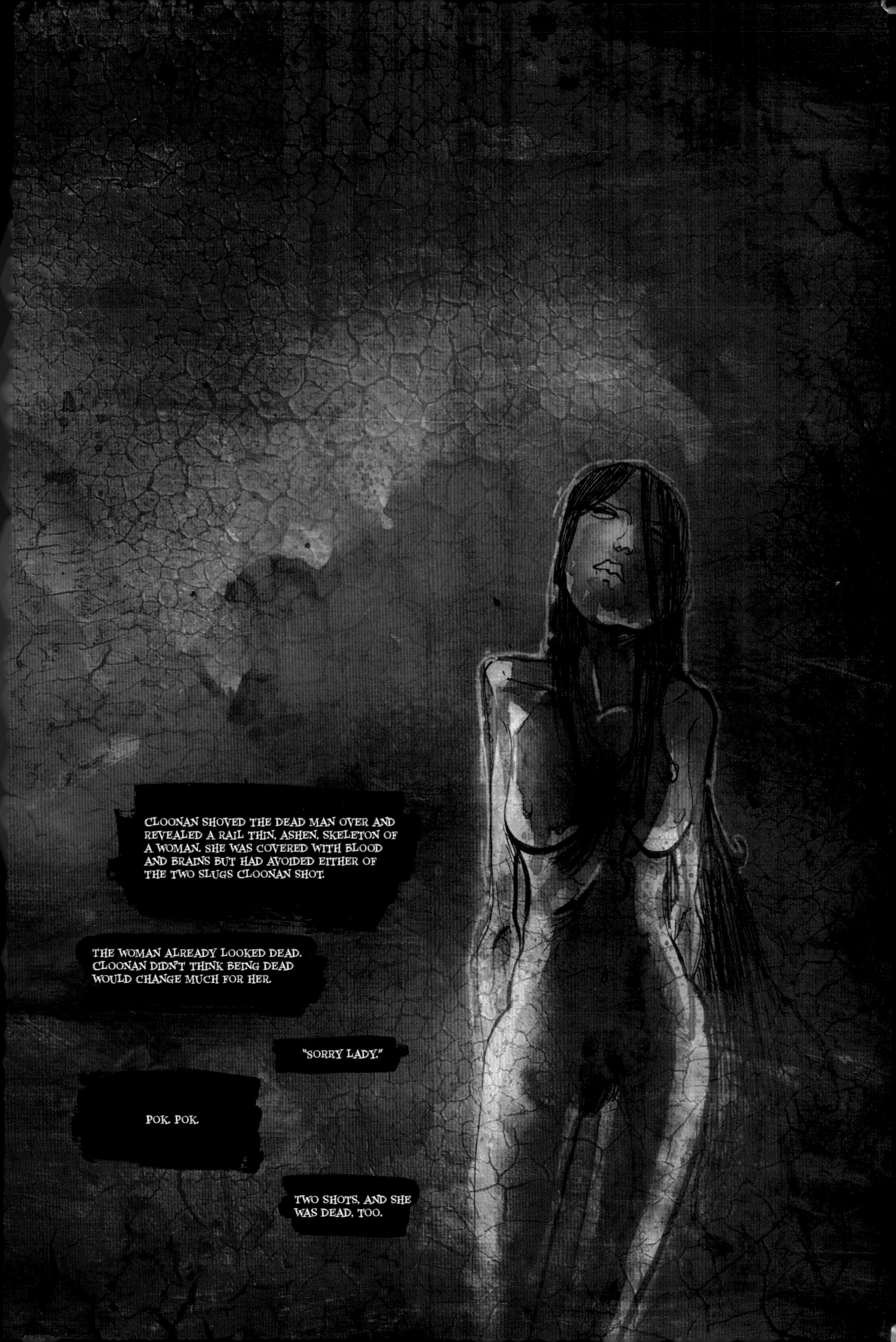
CLOONAN SHOVED THE DEAD MAN OVER AND REVEALED A RAIL THIN, ASHEN, SKELETON OF A WOMAN. SHE WAS COVERED WITH BLOOD AND BRAINS BUT HAD AVOIDED EITHER OF THE TWO SLUGS CLOONAN SHOT.
THE WOMAN ALREADY LOOKED DEAD. CLOONAN DIDN'T THINK BEING DEAD WOULD CHANGE MUCH FOR HER.
"SORRY LADY."
POK. POK.
TWO SHOTS, AND SHE WAS DEAD, TOO.

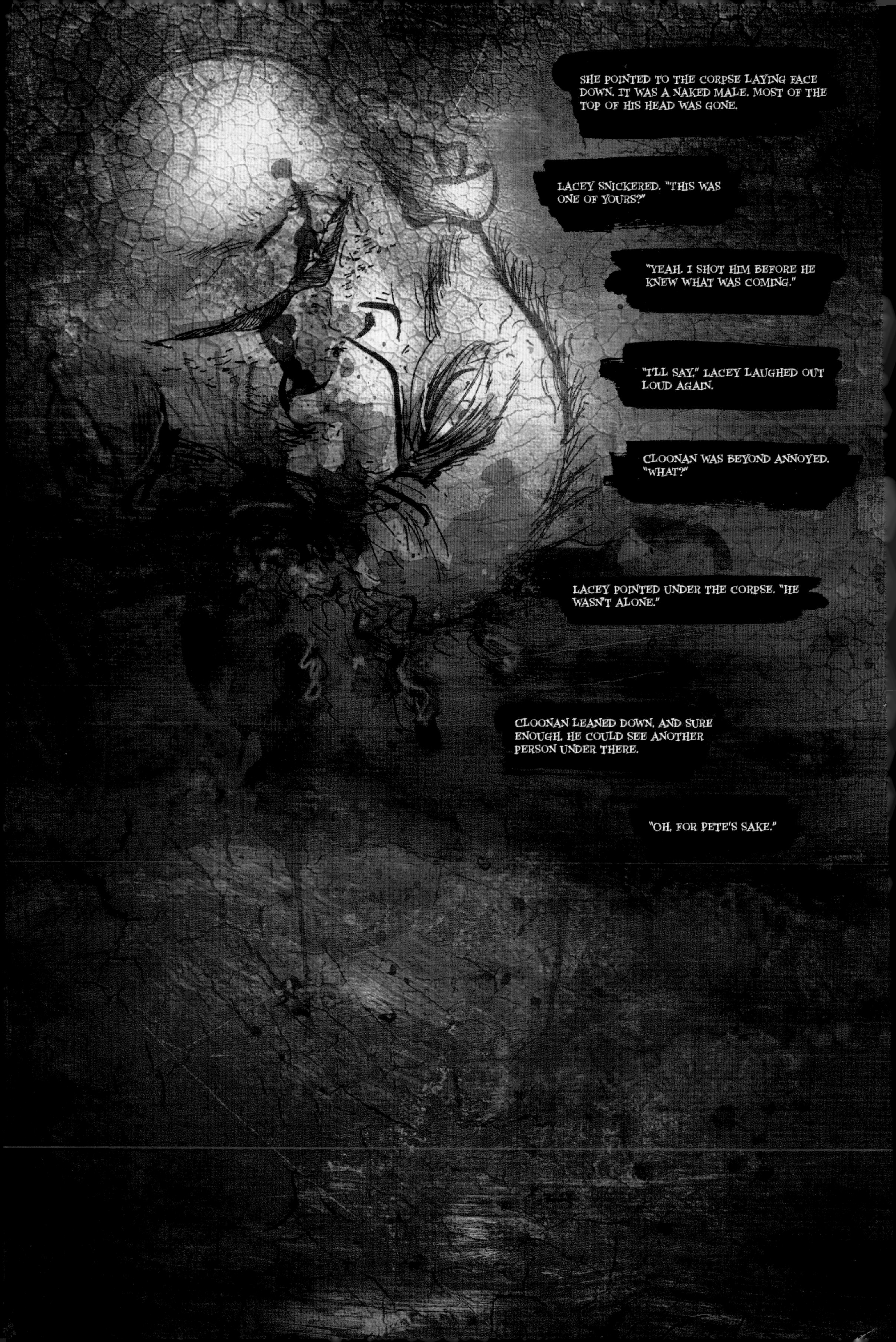
SHE POINTED TO THE CORPSE LAYING FACE DOWN. IT WAS A NAKED MALE. MOST OF THE TOP OF HIS HEAD WAS GONE.
LACEY SNICKERED. "THIS WAS ONE OF YOURS?"
"YEAH. I SHOT HIM BEFORE HE KNEW WHAT WAS COMING."
"I'LL SAY." LACEY LAUGHED OUT LOUD AGAIN.
CLOONAN WAS BEYOND ANNOYED. "WHAT?"
LACEY POINTED UNDER THE CORPSE. "HE WASN'T ALONE."
CLOONAN LEANED DOWN, AND SURE ENOUGH, HE COULD SEE ANOTHER PERSON UNDER THERE.
"OH, FOR PETE'S SAKE."

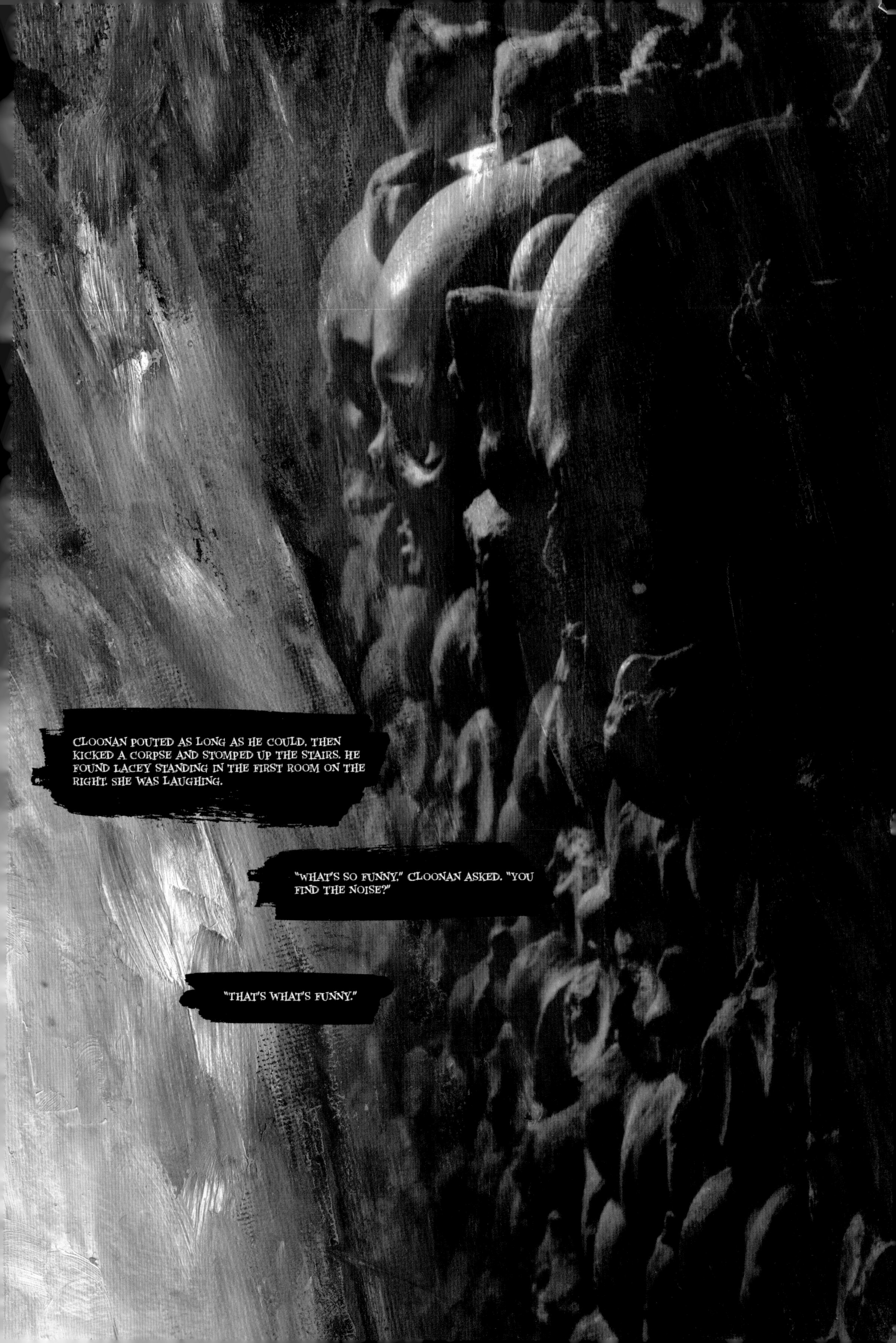
CLOONAN POUTED AS LONG AS HE COULD, THEN KICKED A CORPSE AND STOMPED UP THE STAIRS. HE FOUND LACEY STANDING IN THE FIRST ROOM ON THE RIGHT. SHE WAS LAUGHING.
"WHAT'S SO FUNNY," CLOONAN ASKED. "YOU FIND THE NOISE?"
"THAT'S WHAT'S FUNNY."

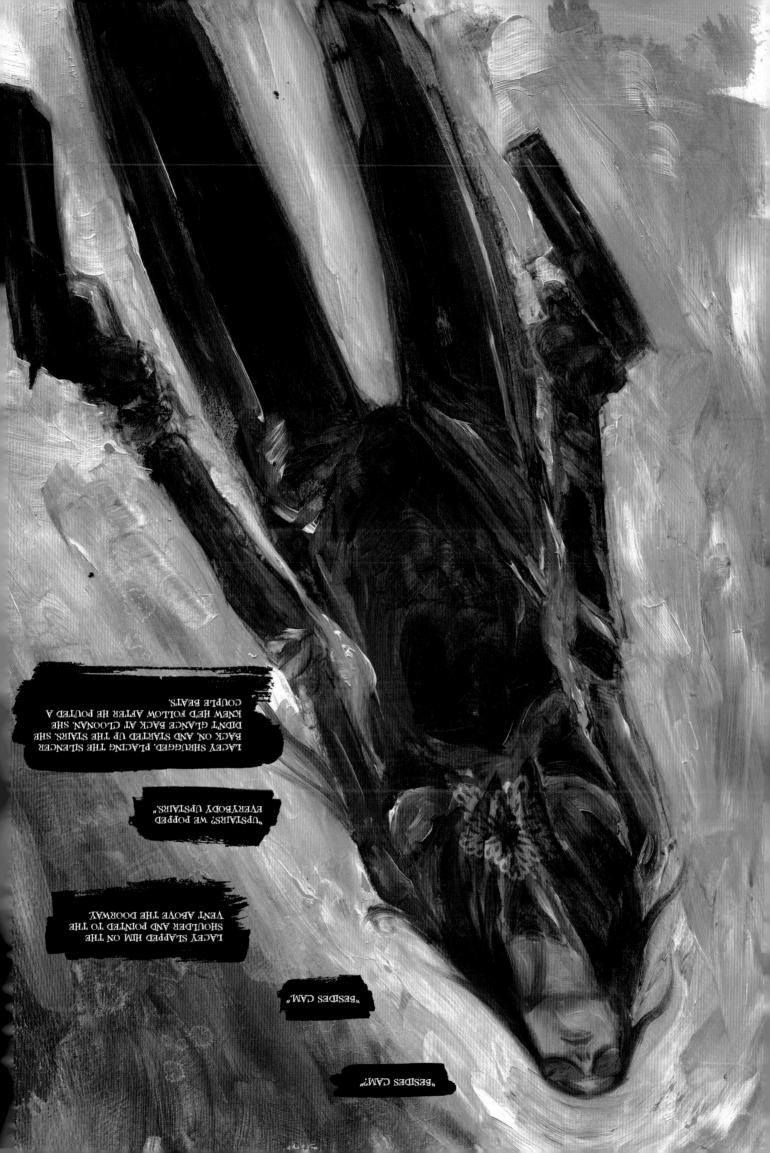

"BESIDES CAM?"

"BESIDES CAM."

LACEY SLAPPED HIM ON THE
SHOULDER AND POINTED TO THE
VENT ABOVE THE DOORWAY.

"UPSTAIRS? WE POPPED
EVERYBODY UPSTAIRS."

LACEY SHRUGGED, PLACING THE SILENCER
BACK ON, AND STARTED UP THE STAIRS. SHE
DIDN'T GLANCE BACK AT CLOONAN. SHE
KNEW HE'D FOLLOW AFTER HE POUTED A
COUPLE BEATS.

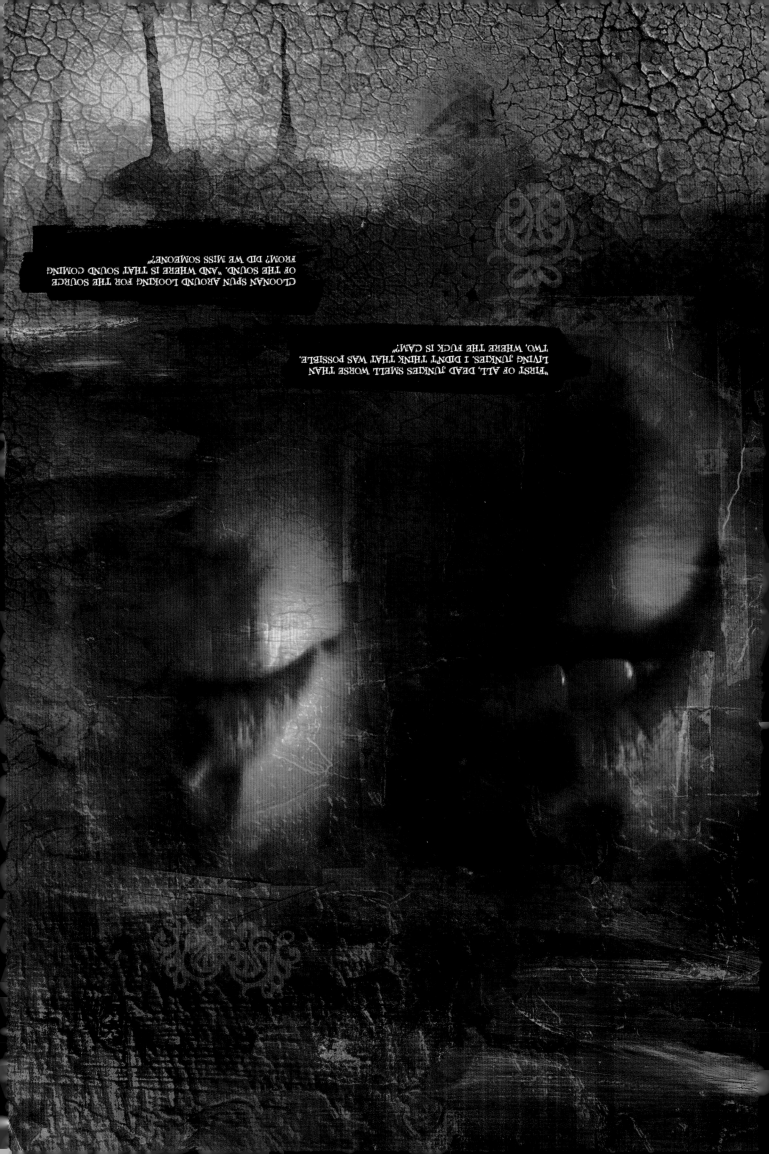

CLOONAN SPUN AROUND LOOKING FOR THE SOURCE OF THE SOUND. "AND WHERE IS THAT SOUND COMING FROM? DID WE MISS SOMEONE?"

"FIRST OF ALL, DEAD JUNKIES SMELL WORSE THAN LIVING JUNKIES. I DIDN'T THINK THAT WAS POSSIBLE. TWO, WHERE THE FUCK IS CAM?"

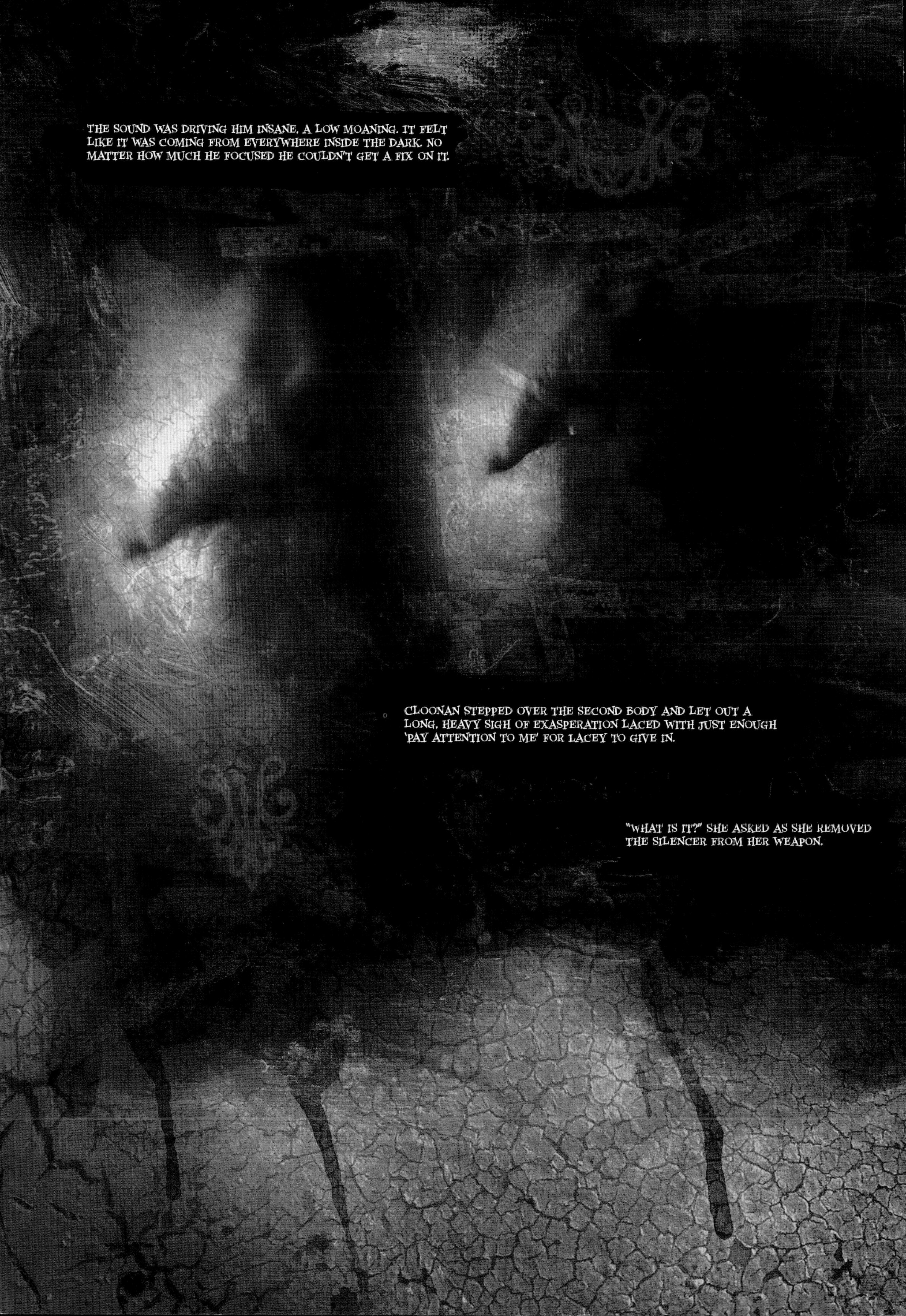
THE SOUND WAS DRIVING HIM INSANE, A LOW MOANING. IT FELT LIKE IT WAS COMING FROM EVERYWHERE INSIDE THE DARK. NO MATTER HOW MUCH HE FOCUSED HE COULDN'T GET A FIX ON IT.
CLOONAN STEPPED OVER THE SECOND BODY AND LET OUT A LONG, HEAVY SIGH OF EXASPERATION LACED WITH JUST ENOUGH 'PAY ATTENTION TO ME' FOR LACEY TO GIVE IN.
"WHAT IS IT?" SHE ASKED AS SHE REMOVED THE SILENCER FROM HER WEAPON.

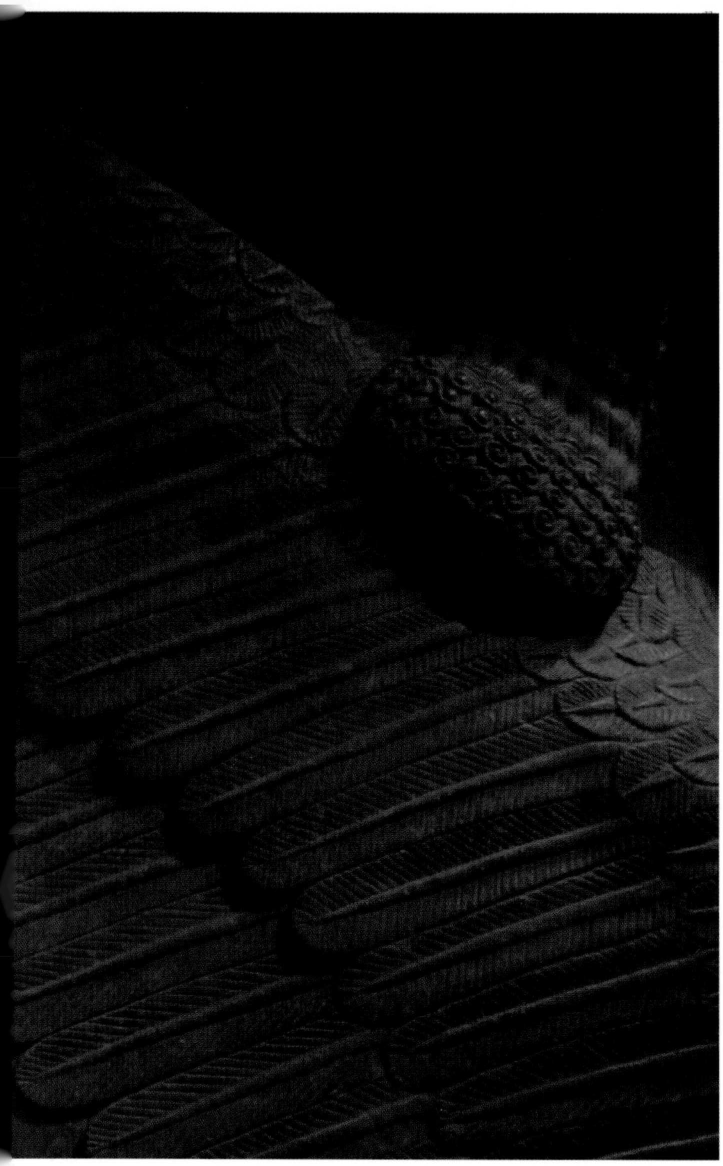

FOREWORD

BY : WARREN ELLIS

What does it feel like?

A hunger for something that is separate from oneself. A want for something that doesn't belong to you. A wish to consume a thing that you believe will make you feel more complete, if only for a moment. A need for that time that will connect you to something else.

We are never more lonely than when in a state of lust. In our need we are exposed, a little animal paralysed by the want for a touch that comes from elsewhere.

What does it feel like, when lust is nothing but failure and disappointment? When we cannot actualise that simplest of concepts: to have something that tastes a little bit like love. Like reciprocation. To be understood as something perhaps worth having for a little while.

There was a man in Britain, Dennis Nilsen, who killed people because he knew he would, sooner or later, be considered unworthy of their desire, and they would leave. He killed them and kept them so that he wouldn't be alone. In the periods where he was without such company, he would lay facing a full-length mirror placed on its side, to create the illusion that there was someone with him in the night, in the sick empty hours where his ability to feel lust meant nothing to anyone.

Lust makes us feel further apart from others than any other experience. Nothing is as distancing as needing someone else so badly that nothing matters more than them needing us in the same way -- and, deep in the tiniest part of our mind, knowing full well that they might not. We have no protection from that person or thing turning around and seeing us for the ugly, lumpen creature we are.

Lust is that moment when we are most alone and closest to the final murder of our heart.

We are burning people, standing on a frozen lake, and beneath the ice familiar monsters coil, waiting for us to fall into the dark.

What does it feel like? Lust is closing your eyes, putting a gun to your lips and hoping to hell that it feels like a kiss.

Warren Ellis

April 2013